MORE *MURDEROUS* MATHS

BY KJARTAN POSKITT

Illustrated by
Philip Reeve

Hippo

To Margaret Fenton, the warmest, wisest and most wonderful person I know – and best of all she's my granny.

Scholastic Children's Books,
Commonwealth House, 1–19 New Oxford Street,
London WC1A 1NU, UK
a division of Scholastic Ltd
London ~ New York ~ Toronto ~ Sydney ~ Auckland
Mexico City ~ New Delhi ~ Hong Kong

First published in this edition by Scholastic Ltd, 1999
First published in the UK by Scholastic Ltd, 1998
Text copyright © Kjartan Poskitt, 1998
Illustrations copyright © Philip Reeve, 1998

ISBN 0 439 01153 1

Typeset by TW Typesetting, Midsomer Norton, Somerset
Printed and bound in Denmark by Nørhaven Paperback, Viborg

10 9

The right of Kjartan Poskitt and Philip Reeve to be identified as
the author and illustrator of this work respectively has been asserted
by them in accordance with the Copyright, Designs and Patents
Act, 1988.

CONTENTS

MORE
MURDEROUS
MATHS

·MURDEROUS MATHS·

JOIN THE MURDEROUS MATHS GANG
FOR MORE FUN, GAMES AND TIPS AT
www.murderousmaths.co.uk

Also by Kjartan Poskitt:

THE STORY SO FAR...

City: Chicago, Illinois, U.S.A.
Place: The state penitentiary
Date: 2 December, 1929
Time: 4:00 a.m.

The dynamite flew in through the bars of the window and rolled across the floor.

"Geez!" screamed One Finger Jimmy. "She's doing it. She's getting us out!"

"Grab some cover!" shouted Blade Bocelli. "That fuse ain't gonna wait!"

The seven men ripped their bunks apart and seconds later were cowering in a corner behind a wall of mattresses.

"Move over, you guys," said the biggest man. "My rear is still exposed."

"What's your problem, Porky?" sneered the Weasel. "With the size of that thing, if you sat on a fork at breakfast, you wouldn't shout ouch until dinner."

"Clam up!" ordered Blade. "And keep down."

Each man screwed his eyes shut tight as the spark spat its way down the fuse.

"Coo-ee boys!" sang a voice from the door. "Sleeping tight, I hope!"

7

A large key clanged in the lock. As the door opened a scent of heavy perfume drifted in and collided with the reek of old socks.

"Dolly Snowlips!" gasped Jimmy. "What you doing there? You're supposed to be waiting over the wall with the pick-up truck."

"Yeah, but that was *your* plan," replied the figure silhouetted in the light from the corridor. "And face it, you guys ain't too smart."

"We is plenty smart enough, sister," said Chainsaw Charlie.

"Oh yeah?" came the reply. "Smart enough to get shot up and arrested all because not one of you seven guys could figure out a restaurant bill?"

"Numbers could have figured it," said Jimmy.

"Seven sevens, 49. Seven 49s, three-four-three. Seven three-four-threes, two-four-o-one..." gibbered the thin man.

"He's just a machine in pants," said Dolly. "Sure, Numbers can do the sums, but he don't know what sums to do!"

"He does what I tell him," said Blade Bocelli. "Remember, inside or out, I'm still the boss."

"That's debatable," said Dolly. "Who's the one hiding in the corner in his underwear?"

"Hey! That's you, boss," said Half-smile Gabrianni.

"And who's the one who's just been in the governor's office having cocktails and bailing you out?"

"We're bailed out?" gasped the mob.

"You mean somebody actually paid money so that we're free to go?" said Blade.

"They sure did," said Dolly. "And that's a whole lot better way of you getting out of here than explosions, sirens and me freezing my knees off in some blacked-out truck with false plates."

"How could we get bail?" said Jimmy. "We're the evilest, meanest, dirtiest dogs that ever did a dastardly deed."

"Yeah, that's us," the rest all chorused.

"That's why bail was ten million bucks," said Dolly.

There was a shocked silence.

"And where did these ten fat ones come from?" asked Blade.

"A friend," said Dolly. "A friend who wants it paid back."

"Where are we supposed to find that sort of dough?"

"The Fort Knocks Wages Express," said Dolly.

"You're joking," gasped Blade. "Nobody knocks off the Knocks Express."

"I got it all figured out," said Dolly.

"Wow!" said Jimmy. "What a dame!"

"Maybe I don't like it," said Blade.

"Maybe no one's asking you," said Chainsaw. "Looks like Doll's the boss now."

"Good," said Dolly. "Well what are you waiting for? Come on."

She turned and set off down the corridor. One by one the bewildered men stepped out to follow her, with the big man at the rear. It was just as he was easing himself through the narrow door that he called out:

"Hey Doll! If you got us bail, and you ain't waiting outside with the truck, what's the gag with chucking the dynamite?"

"I didn't chuck no dynamite," replied Dolly. "Why would I chuck dynamite when I fixed bail?"

"Well somebody chucked dynamite!" said Porky.

Somewhere inside the package on the cell floor, the spark reached the end of its journey.

Yes here we go … with *More Murderous Maths*.

MORE Murderous Maths?

Yes, because there's another book that's just called *Murderous Maths*, so this one is called *More Murderous Maths*. Good grief, does this mean that this book has maths which is even *more* murderous than plain old *Murderous Maths*? Or does it just mean there's more of it?

Who knows?

Who cares?

Maybe it means that you should have read *Murderous Maths* first, because if you read *More Murderous Maths* first, then it won't be more because you haven't read any other Murderous Maths yet?

Actually it doesn't matter whether you've read the first book or not, the point is that maths isn't just dull old sums.

It's about slick tricks and gruesome games, it's about being famous for ever, it's about trying to predict the future, it's about total control of everything that goes on around us...

DEADLY DOMS

So there you are popping back from the shops with a pizza when...

"Aha!" comes an evil voice. "Gotcha!"

Suddenly you find yourself swinging 30 m above the ground. You raise one eyebrow nonchalantly (so that the eyebrow is 30.007 m above the ground). You heave a heavy sigh because this sort of thing is getting tedious.

It turns out that your arch enemy Professor Fiendish has just driven by in a mobile crane and grabbed you with the hook.

"Come with me," he sneers. "This time I've got a puzzle you'll never solve! Har har har!"

Soon you find yourself in a cell which has a skeleton chained to the wall. In front of the skeleton is a chessboard and a box of dominoes.

"There are 32 dominoes in the box," says the mad professor. "And the chessboard has eight squares

13

along each side, which makes 64 squares all together."

You knew that.

"Each domino can cover exactly two squares of the chessboard," says the professor. "So, can you put the 32 dominoes on the board so that every square is covered?"

Easy peasy. You solve the puzzle in a trice.

"Big deal," you say. "Now let me go, my pizza's getting cold."

"Not so fast!" sniggers the professor. "I'm going to chop two squares off the chessboard, and take away one of the dominoes."

The professor takes a knife and chops away two squares from opposite corners of the board. The squares are both white.

"There are now 62 squares left and 31 dominoes," says the professor. "Can you cover all the squares now?"

Obviously the owner of the skeleton couldn't do it, but can you?

Different sorts of 'ominoes

Forget about the spots on dominoes, just have a think about the shape. A domino shape is made up of two little

14

squares joined together. There, that was a quick think, wasn't it?

We'll come back to dominoes later, but in the meantime have another think.

Suppose you only used *one* square, it wouldn't really be a domino would it? In fact you could call it a *monomino*.

Using *two* squares you get a *domino*.

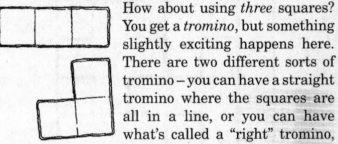 How about using *three* squares? You get a *tromino*, but something slightly exciting happens here. There are two different sorts of tromino – you can have a straight tromino where the squares are all in a line, or you can have what's called a "right" tromino, where the squares make a little corner.

With *four* squares you can make *tetrominoes*, and there are five different types carefully drawn out here by our murderous artist, The Evil Reeve.

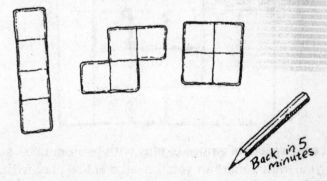

Oh dear. The Reeve has just popped out for a custard sandwich, so you'll have to draw the last two tetrominoes in yourself.

Probably best of all, with *five* squares you can make *pentominoes*.

There are 12 different pentominoes and here you can see they are arranged in a neat 6 × 10 formation. It looks simple, doesn't it?

There are lots of games to play with pentominoes, so if you want some fun you'll need a set to play with. The best and cheapest way to get them is to copy this page on to some card (and make it bigger if you can) then cut out the shapes. It's fun to make each shape a different colour too.

(You can sometimes buy sets of pentominoes in a games shop all nicely made out of wood, or you can also get "Pentominoes" to play on a computer. Look out for it on disks that have lots of little games on.)

So there you are with 12 pentominoes. Here are some wicked challenges for you:

1 Arrange the 12 pentominoes back into a 6 × 10 shape like before. There are 2,339 different ways of doing this, but if you can find more than three or four then you're doing well!

2 Arrange the 12 pentominoes into a 5 × 12 shape. There are 1,010 ways of doing this, but it's quite tricky!

3 Arrange the 12 pentominoes into a 4 × 15 shape. There are 368 ways of doing this. Very tricky!

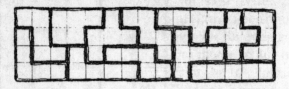

4 Arrange the 12 pentominoes into a 3 × 20 shape. There are only supposed to be two ways of doing this and here's one of them. Can you find the other? (And it doesn't count if your version is just the same as this one flipped over!)

5 Pick any one of the shapes. Using nine of the other shapes, can you can make a big version of the shape you have picked...

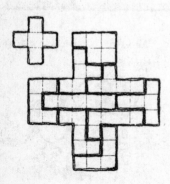

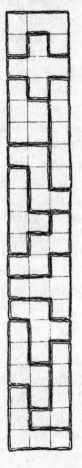

6 Finally, here's a great game to play with a friend. You need your pentominoes and a square board (like a chessboard) marked out with 64 squares so that a pentomino covers five squares.

- The first player picks a pentomino from the set and puts it on the board covering any five squares.

- The other player picks another pentomino and puts it on the board, but it mustn't overlap the first pentomino.

- Keep taking turns until somebody can't go.
- Whoever puts down the last pentomino wins!

A rule to break:

You're not supposed to turn the pentominoes over in any of these puzzles (i.e. you're not supposed to make the shape on the left into the one on the right).

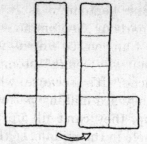

However, the idea of this book is to have fun, so as it's a bit of a petty rule, you can be a mad rebellious anarchist and ignore it. You might even find more solutions to the puzzles!

Enough about pentominoes.

Hexominoes use *six* squares and there are 35 different ones. Here are a few...

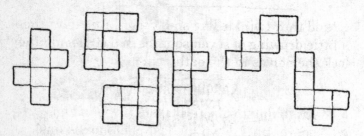

Heptominoes use *seven* squares and there are 108 different ones including...

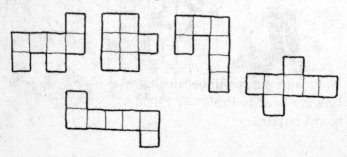

20

One heptomino is rather special. It's called the "harbour" heptomino…

Can you see why it gives maths freaks stomach ache? It's because when they are making patterns up, they can't fill up the hole in the middle, so they end up gibbering away in corners and chewing their toes.

Aren't mathematicians brilliant? Give them an equation like Endean's Determination of the Invariance of the Hubble Constant:

$$T_0 = \frac{2L\left[S_0(T_0) - \operatorname{Sin} S_0(T_0)\right]}{\operatorname{Sin}^2 S_0(T_0)}$$

AHH!

… and they twinkle like snowflakes. But show them a little drawing of seven squares in a circle and they lock themelves in the bathroom.

ARGHH! TAKE IT AWAY! MUMMY!

Well, your pizza will be turning to rubber by now, so let's get back to Professor Fiendish's chopped chessboard puzzle.

The puzzle is impossible, but he will have to let you go if you tell him why. The answer is rather slick!

When you put the dominoes on the chessboard, each domino covers two squares next to each other. This means each domino has to cover one black square and one white square.

After the professor chopped off two white squares, the board was left with 30 white squares and 32 black squares.

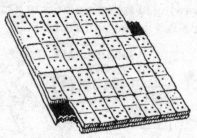

When you've put 30 dominoes on the board, you will have covered up 30 black and 30 white squares. This means the two uncovered squares both have to be black. It doesn't matter how you placed the 30 dominoes, and it doesn't matter where on the board the two uncovered squares are, *they have to be black*.

Obviously there's no way you can cover two black squares with one domino (you're not allowed to break it in half), so the puzzle is impossible!

A FISHY PROBLEM

In the garden at Fogsworth Manor, the Duchess was examining the pond.

"Ah, Croak, there you are," she said as the butler approached. "I've decided to smarten up the pond for Twinkle, my little goldfish."

"What's wrong with it?" asked Croak.

"It needs some railings along the side by the path," said the Duchess. "I don't want Herbert's croquet balls to roll in and frighten her. Let's measure it up."

Croak held the tape at one end of the pond as the Duchess walked down to the other.

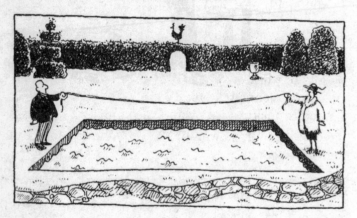

"There!" said the Duchess. "It comes to 12 metres. Go and get 12 metres of railings."

In the hardware shop the manager was fixing up a massive parcel.

"That's all you want, guv?" he said. "Twelve metres of railings?"

"Probably not," said Croak. "But that's all for now."

Back in the garden the railings were in position.

"Perfect!" said the Duchess. "Now then, the bottom of the pond looks a bit murky. I think Twinkle would like it covered in nice pink tiles. See to it, Croak."

In the hardware shop...

"You again?" asked the manager.

"She wants the bottom tiled now," moaned Croak.

"How many tiles?" asked the manager.

"I dunno," said Croak. "It's 12 metres long, you work it out."

"That's no good!" said the manager. "I need to know how wide it is!"

"You didn't need to know for the railings!" said Croak.

"That's 'cos railings is linear, you see. That means they are in a line. Tiles is area. I need two measurements to work out area."

"Two?" moaned Croak.

"You're lucky, mate, you've got a nice rectangular pond. If it was a wonky shape I'd need loads of measurements."

SCRITCH SCROTCH

Croak didn't feel lucky at all, but went back to the Duchess.

"So for tiles we need to know the length *and* the width?" asked the Duchess.

"Apparently so, madam," said Croak.

They got the tape out again.

FIVE METRES WIDE...

Back in the hardware shop...

"So you're saying your pond is 12 metres long by five metres wide?" asked the manager.

"Yes," said Croak.

"Well 12 times five is 60, so the bottom of your pond is 60 square metres," said the manager.

"Square metres?" puzzled Croak. "What's them?"

"Them's *area*," said the manager. "One square metre is the same as a square one metre along each side."

"Oh goody," muttered Croak sarcastically.

"It takes four tiles to cover a square metre, so you need 60 times four which makes 240 tiles," said the manager.

"What I really need is a lorry to carry this lot," moaned Croak as the manager piled up the boxes of tiles.

Eventually the bottom of the pond was tiled.

"Will that be all, madam?" asked Croak.

"Of course not!" said the Duchess. "Twinkle needs some new water."

"I'll get the hose pipe," said Croak.

"Not likely!" said the Duchess. "I'm not having Twinkle swimming about in common tap water. Go and get some posh pond water."

Back in the hardware shop, the manager didn't so much as raise an eyebrow.

"Posh pond water?" he asked. "Of course we sell posh pond water. Very expensive mind you. How much do you want?"

"The pond is 12 metres long by five metres wide," said Croak. "You work it out."

"That's no good!" said the manager. "I need to know how deep it is too."

"But you didn't need to know for the tiles," said Croak.

"That's because tiles is area," said the manager. "Water is volume. I need three measurements to work out volume."

"It's the same depth all over," said Croak hopefully. "There's no shallow end or anything."

"So? I still need to know what the depth is."

"Give me strength!" muttered Croak and once again set off home.

As he went, the manager went to the tap in his backyard and started to fill up lots of bottles. Very carefully he wrote on each one "posh pond water".

"Posh pond water indeed!" smirked the manager. "I'll be selling her ladyship posh air to breathe next."

Back home the Duchess was bewildered.

"So for water, we need to know the length *and* the width *and* the depth?" asked the Duchess.

"It seems so, m'lady," said Croak.

The Duchess tied a stone to the end of the tape, then dangled it down into the pond.

"This is all very niggling," she muttered. "There, it's one-and-a-half metres."

For the fifth time Croak went back to the hardware shop. His feet were killing him.

"Twelve times five times one-and-a-half," said the

manager. "That comes to 90 cubic metres."

"What's a cubic metre?" asked Croak, then immediately wished he hadn't.

"Cubic is volume," said the manager. "And a cubic metre is like a square box shape, which is one metre long, one metre wide and one metre high."

"Oh, brilliant," said Croak. "Not only do my feet hurt, now you're making my brain hurt."

"That's nothing," sniggered the manager. "One cubic metre is the same as 1,000 litres, so if your pond is 90 cubic metres, that makes 90,000 litres."

"What's a litre?" asked Croak.

"That's how much pond water you get in a bottle," said the manager. "Are you carrying these bottles home?"

"I suppose so," said Croak.

"Oh dear," sniggered the manager. "Because that means you'll have to carry 90,000 of them."

"*What?*" gasped Croak.

"And as 1,000 litres of water weighs a tonne, that's 90 tonnes you'll be carrying. Your arms will be hurting too!"

After many many trips from the hardware store back to the pond, the last bottle was finally tipped in.

"Look here, Twinkle!" cooed the Duchess, clutching a rather bored goldfish in a bowl. "Look what Mummy's got for her little treasure..."

The goldfish peered towards the pond.

"Well?" simpered the Duchess. "Isn't it lovely?"

Twinkle yawned and turned away. Croak gave her a murderous look. He guessed what was coming next...

"Doesn't Twinkle like her pond?" asked the Duchess. "Does she prefer her cosy little bowl? That's all right then, Croak can fill it all in and make us a nice summer-house instead."

Line, area, volume – what is it all about? Why do you sometimes need more measurements than others? Look at this road...

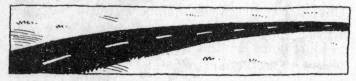

Suppose you run right along it – how far do you go? Does it depend on:

- how long the road is? (Yes – 300 metres)
- how wide the road is? (No)
- how deep the road's foundations are? (No)

The answer only needs *one* number – this is called a *line* or *linear* measurement, e.g. 300 metres.

Suppose you have to paint the whole surface of the road. How much painting do you need to do? Does it depend on:

- how long the road is? (Yes – 300 metres)
- how wide the road is? (Yes – 4 metres)
- how deep the road's foundations are? (No)

This answer needs *two* numbers (which are then usually multiplied together) – this gives an *area* measurement. In this case it works out to be: $300 \times 4 = 1,200$ square metres.

Suppose you have to dig up the whole road. How much digging do you need to do? Does it depend on:

- how long the road is? (Yes – 300 metres)
- how wide the road is? (Yes – 4 metres)
- how deep the road's foundations are? (Yes – so we'd better check)

THE FOUNDATIONS ARE TWO METRES DEEP

This answer needs *three* numbers (which are then usually multiplied together). This gives a *volume* measurement. In this case you'd have to dig up $300 \times 4 \times 2$ which comes to 2,400 cubic metres.

Luckily, we never need more than three measurements because we live in a three-dimensional world. WARNING: Before reading on, fix a smoke alarm to your head. If it goes off, it means your brain is overheating.

OK, here we go! It's time to leap into the unknown and consider...

A question of dimensions *or*, Who can see you stark naked even as you read this book?

To explain the three-dimensional (or 3-D) world for you, please welcome the Fabulous Tightsov brothers.

First of all, they are going to demonstrate life in one dimension.

What these guys are trying to show is that in one dimension everything happens in a line, and if you want to move, you can move only along that line.

Here's a more accurate 1-D world:

Not much to it, is there? If you want to draw a 1-D person in the 1-D world, then get a very sharp pencil and mark a tiny dot on the line. If your person wanted to move about, they could only move along the line, they can't run across the rest of the page or jump out of the book!

Sorry, that was getting a bit strange, so we'll forget it and move on.

Life in two dimensions would be a bit easier...

With life in two dimensions, you have a flat area to move about on, but you can't float above it or sink underneath it. Mind you, this flat area doesn't have to be horizontal, it could be tipped up at any angle…

As the brothers are kindly showing us by clinging on, it doesn't matter what angle the flat area is at, in 2-D you have to stay on it.

We'll take a closer look at life in 2-D in a minute, but before we do we'll let the brothers show us life in 3-D.

In three dimensions, you're not stuck to the 2-D flat area anymore – you can get away from it!

Because we are so used to living in three dimensions, it is very hard to imagine anything else, but just for fun, let's go back to thinking what two dimensions would be like.

Life in 2-D

The main thing about living in two dimensions is that everything would be flat. Do you know how flat you would be in a two-dimensional world? Guess:

- exactly one metre
- one millimetre
- the thickness of a hair
- even flatter than that.

If you want to know the answer then get ready, because this takes some imagining.

Suppose you were a 2-D person and there was a single piece of paper lying next to you. You wouldn't be able to look over the edge of the paper because you would be *so* flat!

This is because even paper has three dimensions, although one of its dimensions (the thickness) is very

PEEP PEEP PEEP

small. What's more, since paper has three dimensions, you can put one piece on top of another. Isn't that just fantastic? (If you are a 2-D creature, this is completely incomprehensible. Even something as silly as playing leap-frog is just too freakish for words.)

So why can't two-dimensional things be on top of each other? Luckily there is one thing we all know about that is two-dimensional – and that is a shadow. Try this:

1 Hold your hands under a strong light so they cast a shadow on the wall.

2 Move one hand behind the other, so the shadows overlap. Can you tell which hand's shadow is on top of the other?

Of course not, because neither is on top. What's more, it doesn't matter if you make your shadows on the floor or the wall or even the ceiling – whichever way up they are, they have only two dimensions.

AT LEAST I UNDERSTOOD THE SHADOW BIT!

Views in different dimensions

If you were living in one-dimension land then you would be just a dot, but what could you see? Get a bit of card and put a pinhole in it. Look through it, but don't hold it too close to your eye. All you can see through the hole is a tiny little speck, and that's what the view in a 1-D world is like. If there was nobody there, then the speck would be blank.

If there was somebody else living in your one dimension, they would look like another dot and they would be straight in front of you because they have to be on the line too.

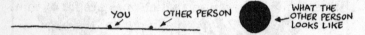

Suppose there was a whole crowd of people in one-dimension land, this is how they would look...

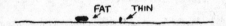

You can't see over or around the person nearest you, so all you would see is that person. That's why going to the cinema in one-dimension land is so frustrating – if just one person sits in front of you, they'll completely and totally block your view.

Fashion conscious people would love living in 1-D land, because it doesn't matter if you're fat or thin ...

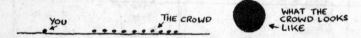

... to any other 1-D person looking at you, you'll still look like this:

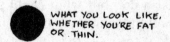

WHAT YOU LOOK LIKE, WHETHER YOU'RE FAT OR THIN.

OK, it's getting strange again, so let's move on.

In a two-dimensional world, your view is rather different. To get a rough idea of what it's like, cut a long narrow slit in some cardboard. Have a look through it – all you can see of the world is a thin line. At least that's better than in 1-D when all you could see was a pinpoint! What's interesting though is that through the narrow slit in your cardboard, you can see the one-dimensional world and in fact you have a much better view of it than a 1-D person because you can see the whole crowd of 1-D people at once. You can even tell which ones are fat or thin.

Here are some 2-D people living on this page:

Peter, Jack and Tom can all see each other because in the 2-D world, they can look around to the right and left. None of them can see Anna because she is in her house and the walls are in the way.

There, that's a bit more straightforward, isn't it? There's one important thing to realize though –

because we are 3-D people, when we look at the 2-D world we can see all four of the 2-D people – even Anna who is in her house! In fact we can see inside and outside Anna's house at the same time.

PEEP PEEP PEEP PEEP DING -A- LING

INSIDE *AND* OUTSIDE– AT THE SAME TIME?!

Relax a minute – and imagine what it would be like to live in a 3-D world.

Well, that's where we do live, so that was easy, wasn't it?

PHEW!

Just remember though:

● A 2-D person can see the whole of a 1-D world.
● A 3-D person can see the whole of a 2-D world.
Therefore, if there is such a thing...
● A 4-D person can see the whole of a 3-D world.

4-D people
Gosh! What does a four-dimensional person look like?

You probably think a 4-D person is impossible, but why should it be?

A flat 2-D person would be very unlikely to recognize or even see a lumpy 3-D person. (Remember 2-D people only have a thin line of vision, and things easily get in the way.) Consequently, 2-D people wouldn't even realize that 3-D people like us exist.

Therefore it follows that we 3-D people are very unlikely to recognize or even see a 4-D person. For all we know, there could be millions of them!

People have tried to work out how the fourth dimension could exist, and some of them say it is *time*. This may sound completely batty, but it shows you how hard it is to imagine anything other than the three dimensions we are used to. Mind you, time does seem an odd sort of dimension because the other three (height, width and depth) can be measured with a ruler. How can you measure time with a ruler? Unless it's a four-dimensional ruler of course...

Calm down, we're nearly finished. There's just one more bit to go, then we'll have some groovy optical illusion pictures which are always good for some fun.

Here's the spookiest part, as we said before. If there are such things as 4-D people, then they can see the whole of our 3-D world at once! In the same way that we can see the inside and outside of Anna's house, they can see the inside and outside of our houses, our rooms and even our clothes. There could be millions of 4-D people who can see you stark naked even right now as you're reading this book! They can even see all your insides working and everything!

There is one small consolation here. If there are 4-D people, then there are probably some 5-D people who can see the 4-D people stark naked, and some 6-D people who can see the 5-D people stark naked and so on...

Mixing dimensions

The good news is that there is some fun to be had in mixing dimensions – in particular if you try and show the 3-D world in 2-D. In other words pictures of solid objects can be a bit strange!

Look at these objects carefully. At first glance

there seems to be nothing wrong with them, and no reason why they couldn't exist in 3-D. But when you study them closely...

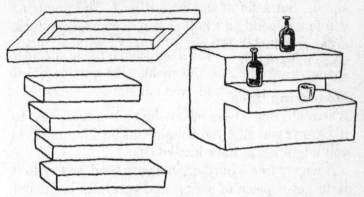

One of the most famous people to use these sorts of illusions was the artist M. C. Escher, and here's a picture of his famous staircase! How would you like to walk up it?

MURDEROUS MEASUREMENTS

You would think measuring things was pretty simple, but a lot of the time it isn't. The problems you face depend on whether you're measuring lines, areas or volumes, but happily there are a few cheaty ways to help you.

Measuring lines
A straight line – easy peasy. Just put a ruler next to it. (Aren't you glad you bought this book? Otherwise you might never have known that.)

A wiggly line – harder! One very good way to do it is to get a piece of string and carefully lay it out along your wiggly line. When you've done that, cut the string to the right length, or mark it where the two ends of the line are. You can then take your string away, pull it straight and hold it against a ruler and measure it.

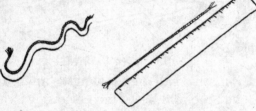

Measuring areas
Some areas are easy peasy and others are tuffy wuffy.

To work areas out you need to do some measuring then use special sums called *formulas*. Wow – formulas sound dead posh, don't they? Actually a lot of them are simple, but they look good and people will think you're really brainy if you can understand them.

Formulas – a good way to be lazy!

The best thing about formulas is that instead of having to write long words out all the time, you can be lazy and just write out a few letters. Let's have a look at the bottom of the Duchess's pond again. Rather usefully it's in the shape of a rectangle, which means three things:

1 All the corners in a rectangle are nice and square.

2 The two long sides are the same length as each other.

3 The two short sides are the same length as each other.

This makes the area dead easy to work out, but before we start, here's a plan of the pond and we'll call the length of the long side "a" and the length of the short side "b".

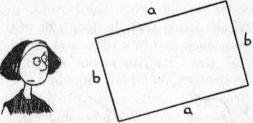

In fact you could call the two lengths anything you like such as Fred and Betty, but because we can't be bothered to write more than we need we'll keep it to "a" and "b".

If we didn't use a formula we'd have to write down: *The area of the rectangle is the length of one of its long sides times the length of one of its short sides.*

Pretty tedious, eh? That's why we use formulas. Instead of putting "the length of one of its long sides" we just put "a", and instead of putting "the length of one of its short sides" we just put "b". This gives us:

The area of a rectangle is "a" times "b".

Of course we can make it even simpler and put the times sign and an equals sign to get:

The area of a rectangle = a × b.

Now here's the *really* lazy bit! Because so many formulas use "times", people don't even bother putting the times sign in, they just put the two letters together that need multiplying:

The area of a rectangle = ab

(You have to be a bit careful which letters you choose here. Suppose you invented a secret formula which multiplied three things that you called "b", "u", and "m", you would end up with secret formula = bum.)

Anyway, now you've got your formula, you have to do some measuring. When the Duchess measured her pond she found that the long side of the pond (which we called "a") was 12 m, and the short side (called "b") was 5 m. This means we can swap the letters in the formula for our numbers:

Area of the pond = a × b = 12 × 5 (which

works out to 60 square metres)

A square area is even easier to work out than a rectangle because the sides are all the same length. Look at this one:

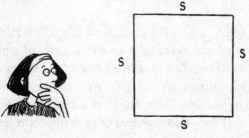

Because the sides are all the same length, we can mark them both with the same letter. This time we've used "s" for square. And why not?

You could write out the area as:

Area of square = s × s, or even "ss"

But there's another way of doing it. If you want to multiply a number by itself, you just need to put a little "2" in the corner after it. This means the number is "squared".

Area of square = s^2

You need to measure only one side – let's say it comes to 7 metres. You can then work out the area of the square:

Area of the square = s × s = 7 × 7 = 49 square metres

By now you'll be itching to get your hands on some decent formulas that will baffle people, so let's turn up the heat and get cooking...

The area for a triangle has a slightly better formula which is this:

$\dfrac{bh}{2}$ (which means the same as b × h ÷ 2)

In formulas a line underneath always means "divided by".

Of course you need to know what "b" and "h" are, so here's a picture to show you:

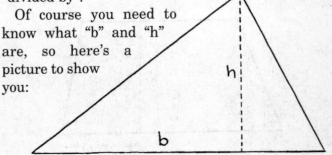

47

"b" is the length of the base of the triangle, and "h" is the height of the triangle going straight upwards. Suppose you found that "b" was 9 cm and "h" was 8 cm, the area of the triangle would be:

$9 \times 8 \div 2 = 36$ square cm

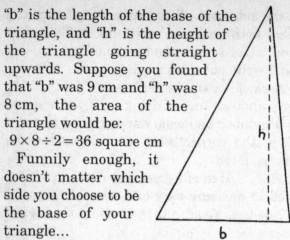

Funnily enough, it doesn't matter which side you choose to be the base of your triangle...

(This is a picture of the same triangle turned round.)

When you measure "b" and "h" then work out the area, you will get the same answer! For instance in this case you might find "b" was 6 cm and "h" was 12 cm. If you put these into your formula you get:

$6 \times 12 \div 2 = 36$ square cm

Clever things formulas, aren't they?

Here's another shape with a formula.

Suppose your rectangle wasn't really a rectangle because one of the sides was too short? It might look like this:

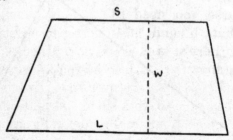

(By the way, this shape is called a *trapezium*. Don't you just *love* words with a letter "z" in the middle?)

First you have to measure the long side (L), the short side (S) and the width straight across (W). The formula for the area is:

$$\frac{(L+S)W}{2},$$ or if you want to put the signs in:
$$(L+S) \times W \div 2$$

The brackets are starting to make this look really tricky, aren't they? Actually, all the brackets mean is that you have to work out the bit inside the brackets first, as you'll see in a minute.

Suppose we measure up and find $L = 10$ cm $S = 6$ cm and $W = 5$ cm. We can put the numbers in the formula:

$$\frac{(10+6) \times 5}{2}$$

Do the sum in the brackets first, so $10 + 6 = 16$. The formula turns into:

$$\frac{16 \times 5}{2},$$ which is $80 \div 2$ which equals 40 square centimetres!

Maybe you've heard about secret formulas in spy films and thought they would be murderously hard to work out. In fact, as long as you know what the letters stand for, if *you* discover any secret formulas, you might be able to work them out yourself! Later on you'll meet some really mega formulas that maybe even your teacher won't know about.

Anyway, going back to working out areas: most areas with straight sides like triangles and rectangles are quite easy – even this one:

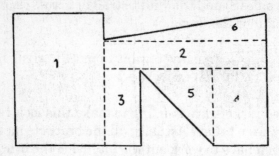

As you can see, all you need to do is divide it up into triangles and rectangles, then you find out how big each part is and finally add them all together.

If shapes have curved sides then they get harder to work out, although if it's a circle then you can use formulas which include a rather groovy thing called "pi" which sounds like "pie", but doesn't taste like pie, and looks like this: π.

No time to tell you here, but point your face at the chapter on "strange numbers", and you'll find out.

If you don't feel up to using measuring and formulas, you'll be glad to know that there's a cheaty way to measure even the toughest areas. All you do is draw your shape on squared paper (and your shape can be as wibbly as you like). You then count up the squares inside the shape. You'll probably end up with some chopped squares at the edge of your shape – the rule is only count them if they look bigger than half a square.

If you really want an accurate measure, instead of using squares of 1 cm × 1 cm, you could use tiny squares such as 1 mm × 1 mm – but you'll have a lot more counting to do!

Gosh, can you smell something funny? A sort of Brussels sprouty fishy cowpatty smell? It's as if somebody with really smelly breath has been studying this page very carefully. Maybe it's just in your imagination – but maybe not. Never mind, let's go on...

Measuring volumes

Measuring volumes can be really tricky unless you're dealing with a nice cuboid shape – in other words a box with eight square corners like a corn-flakes box. In this case you just measure the length, the width and the depth and multiply them all together – again in the same way as the Duchess worked out how much water she needed for her pond. If you want to use a formula it looks like this:

Volume = lwd

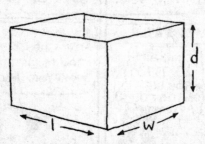

Any volume shapes other than cuboid can be dead tough. If you have circles involved (say you're measuring a ball or tin can) you can work out volumes by using that odd looking π thing, but what do you do if you want to measure the volume of something completely wonky like your foot? You have to grit your teeth, spend several years studying integral calculus and then really set to it.

Oo-er! Happily there's a much funnier way so get ready for the feature you've been waiting all your life to read...

How to measure the volume of your foot

You need:
● a big bowl or bucket
● a foot
● a measuring jug
● a large tray
● some very understanding friends.

PUT THE BOWL ON THE TRAY AND FILL IT TO THE VERY TOP WITH WATER...

TAKE YOUR SHOE AND SOCK OFF...

SLOWLY PUT YOUR FOOT IN THE BOWL. SOME WATER WILL SPLOSH OVER THE EDGE ONTO THE TRAY. THIS WATER IS IMPORTANT SO MAKE SURE YOU CATCH IT ALL...

WHAT ARE YOU DOING?

SOME MURDEROUS MATHS!

ER... WE UNDERSTAND.

YOU DON'T LOOK LIKE A RIGHT NINNY AT ALL...

HONEST!

POUR THE WATER THAT HAS SPILT ONTO THE TRAY INTO THE MEASURING JUG.

SEE HOW MUCH WATER IS IN THE MEASURING JUG - THAT'S THE SAME VOLUME AS YOUR FOOT! (IF THE JUG IS MARKED IN MILLILITRES THEN THAT'S THE SAME AS CUBIC CENTIMETRES)

THERE! THAT'S A LOT EASIER THAN MESSING ABOUT WITH TONS OF MEASUREMENTS AND FORMULAS INVOLVING WEIRD LITTLE THINGS LIKE π, EH?

DOCTOR? WE'RE VERY WORRIED ABOUT OUR FRIEND!

PONG

WHIFF

54

Gosh! There's that awful Brussels sprouty fishy cowpatty smell again! Can you smell it? Oh no! No wonder there's such a horrid smell – it's Professor Fiendish – he's read this book and put in an extra bit...

Dear Reader

HAR HAR! Hello peanut brains, it's Fiendish here! So you think you know all about measuring things now, do you? Eh? EH? Well, if you're so clever, try this one:

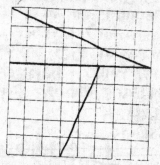

You can see this shape has eight squares along one side and eight squares along the other side, so if you count them all up you'll find the area comes to 64 squares.

PTO ➜➜

Now then, cut along the thick lines and re-arrange the pieces into this pattern...

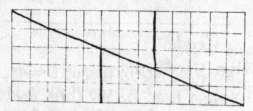

Done that? Now you'll see the shape has thirteen squares along one side and five squares along the other. Work it out (or count them all up if you're a bit of a dur-dur). Either way, you get an area of **65** squares!

So, smarty-pants – **Where did the extra square come from?**

Hah Hah Hah!

Yours smugly **Fiendish**

(Professor Fiendish PHD. MA. OXEN. CBE. BSE)

Oh dear! Does this mean that everything about measuring areas in this chapter is suddenly wrong? The best way to find out is to get some squared paper and copy out the first diagram. Cut out the pieces very carefully and see if you can make the second diagram without leaving any gaps!

MEANWHILE IN THE CITY INFIRMARY...

Porky had visitors.

"Sure was kind of you to save our lives like that," said Weasel.

"Yeah, if you hadn't absorbed the blast, we'd never have made it down the corridor," said Half-smile.

Porky had never been the hero before, and he felt good all over (except for his bottom which felt very sore).

A pair of high heels clicked across the tiles towards them.

"OK boys, break it up," said Dolly. "It's time to go to work."

"Says who?" replied Blade.

"Says the ten million dollars you owe," said Dolly. "With interest."

"I ain't interested in interest," said Blade.

The others all sniggered. Feeble as it was, it was one of Blade's better jokes.

"Yeah," said Jimmy. "Some sucker wants to bail us for ten fat ones, that's his problem."

"Think it through, dummies," said Dolly. "You don't mess around with a guy who can put up that much lettuce. He'll have you straight back inside, and now your cell's blown up, the only place for you will be in Grimstate Pen. You've heard of Grimstate Pen, I take it?"

They had. It was the kind of place where new inmates were recognized because they still had both ears, the Governor had tattooed teeth and the guard dogs were long-nosed, short-legged, African hunting hounds. (Following the unexplained disappearance of several visitors, the authorities avoided using the word "crocodile".)

"Every meal is leftovers from the meal before!" wailed Porky. "There's one potato there that has been dished up three times a day for the last 19 years."

"So how many times is that?" asked Dolly.

"How should I know?" asked Porky.

"It's just simple maths!" said Dolly. "Three times 365 times 19."

"Two-o-eight-o-five," snapped Numbers.

"Maths is for cissies," said Blade. "Who needs it?"

"The interest on this ten million is 15 per cent every week," said Dolly. "So every day you do nothing, you owe more money."

"Every day?" gasped Blade. "How much more?"

"If you want to know, be a cissy and work it out," said Dolly.

With a bored sigh she opened her handbag and checked her lipstick in a vanity mirror. The mob all put their heads together and started to mutter.

Dolly couldn't bear it any more.

"Roll over, big guy," she ordered.

"What for?" moaned Porky.

"I need a drawing-board."

The big man eased himself round in his bed to reveal the massive expanse of white bandage which encased his rear.

"Listen up," said Dolly. "Fifteen per cent interest a week means that for every hundred dollars you owe, after one week you have to pay an extra $15."

"Is that all?" sneered Blade. "A lousy 15 bucks a week?"

Dolly wrote the figures out in lipstick on the big man's bandages.

"That's if you owed a hundred dollars," said Dolly. "But you owe ten million. How many lots of a hundred is that?"

"One hundred thousand," snapped Numbers. "One 0-0-0-0-0."

"And we have to pay $15 interest on every one of those?" asked the Weasel.

"That's right," said Dolly. "So for every week..."

"One million, five hundred thousand dollars of interest," interrupted Numbers.

"OK, you made your point," said Blade. "We start work tomorrow."

"Are you sure you can afford to wait?" said Dolly. "That works out as over $200,000 interest every day. This time tomorrow you'll be nearly a quarter of a million poorer."

"We start today," said Chainsaw. "I might not know much about maths, but I know about being broke and that's what we're gonna be if we don't get moving!"

"Good," said Dolly. "Get down to the freight yard. I'll see you in the signal box in one hour."

SPEED

Here are some speeds:

- The fastest human sprinters can do about 10 metres per second (10 m/s).

- Light travels at 300,000 kilometres per second (300,000 km/s).

- The fastest land animal is the cheetah which can run at about 100 kilometres per hour (100 km/h).

- A really turbo-charged snail might just reach 50 metres per hour (50 m/h).

- New York is moving away from London at about 20 millimetres per year, thanks to what's called continental drift. (No wonder air fares keep going up with planes having to fly further.)

So if they all had a race, who'd win?

It's all a murderous mix-up, isn't it? Are kilometres per second faster than metres per hour? Do millimetres per year outstrip metres per second? In other words, which speed is the fastest?

Speed is pretty simple. There's only one thing you need to know about it and it's this:

Speed is the *distance* you move divided by the *time* it takes

In the last chapter we found out about formulas, so if we want to be lazy we can just put:

$$\text{Speed} = \frac{\text{Distance}}{\text{Time}}, \text{ or even } S = \frac{D}{T}$$

When you see a speed like "ten kilometres per hour" it just says that if you want to go ten kilometres, then it will take you one hour.

OK, now get ready for a deep question...

What is the meaning of "per"?

"Per" is a funny little word, because although everybody uses it when talking about speeds, hardly anybody knows exactly what it means. Try asking a few people, "What does per mean?" and they will go blank and start mumbling.

It's also one of those words that means nothing on its own. If you stand up on a crowded bus and shout "Oranges!", then people might think you're a bit odd, but at least they know what oranges are. On the other hand, if you stand up on a bus and shout "Per!" a few times, nobody will have the foggiest what you're talking about. In fact, the chances are that everybody will quietly move to the back and get off at the next stop.

If you look it up, *per* means "for each", so if you

move at 30 km *per* hour that means you move 30 kilometres *for each* hour you travel. Another way of understanding "per" is to treat it as a cute way of saying "divided by" and if you're writing it for short you just put a "/" sign, which is a little dividing line.

Suppose you could rollerblade along at a speed of 28 kilometres per *two* hours? Sounds a bit odd, doesn't it? There's nothing actually wrong with it, it's just that you don't expect any numbers after the "per". All you need to do to sort it out is remember that speed is distance divided by time. If you write out "28 km per two hours" like a sum you get:

$$\text{Rollerblading speed} = \frac{28 \text{ km}}{2 \text{ hours}}$$

Simple. Just divide the bottom into the top and get:

$$\text{Roller blading speed} = \frac{14 \text{ km}}{1 \text{ hour}}, \text{ which is 14 km per hour or 14 km/h}$$

One thing to be aware of: when talking about speeds people often say things like "50 kilometres *an* hour" or if they talk fast they say "50 kilometres n'our". What they really mean is "50 kilometres per hour".

ONCE AGAIN WE INTERRUPT YOU FOR A FURTHER BULLETIN ON THE GOLLARK AVENGERS...

INTELLIGENCE REPORTS THAT THE ALIEN BATTLE CRUISER CAN ADVANCE AT A TOP SPEED OF **180 GLOMPS** PER **MNULT**!

RUMBBBLE

KZAP!

PTOOi

GOOD GRIEF! THAT SOUNDS FAST! WE'RE ALL **DOOMED**!

WE'LL GIVE YOU FURTHER INFORMATION WHEN WE HAVE IT. IN THE MEANTIME THE PUBLIC ARE ASKED NOT TO PANIC, SO RELAX, SMILE, THINK SWEET THOUGHTS AND LET'S HAVE SOME MORE MURDEROUS MATHS...

Let's go back to our silly race with everything going at different sorts of speeds. If you look carefully, it's obvious that some are faster than others, but the secret is finding out how to compare them. You do this by choosing which sort of speed you like the best and altering all the others to fit it.

Let's choose "metres per second" to be our favourite speed, and for short we'll write it like this: m/s.

First of all we were told that a sprinter can reach

10 m/s. Hooray, we don't need to change that one.

Next we're told that light travels at 300,000 kilometres per second. As one kilometre = 1,000 metres, obviously 300,000 kilometres is the same as 300,000,000 metres.

This means we can say that light travels at 300,000,000 m/s.

After that, we found out that the fastest land animal is the cheetah which can run at about 100 kilometres per hour. Just as we did before we change the kilometres to metres, so we get: cheetahs run at 100,000 metres per hour.

Hang on! That's no good. If we want to compare cheetahs to everything else, we need to know how many metres they can run per second. To work it out, we'll write this speed like a sum. (Remember that speed equals distance divided by time.)

$$\text{Cheetah speed in metres per hour} = \frac{100,000 \text{ metres}}{1 \text{ hour}}$$

Now we need to know how many seconds there are in an hour, but that's not too hard. There are 60 minutes in an hour, and each minute has 60 seconds, so in one hour there are 60×60 seconds which comes to 3,600. Now we can swap the hour in our sum for seconds:

$$\text{Cheetah speed in metres per second} = \frac{100,000 \text{ metres}}{3,600 \text{ seconds}}$$

So now you can work it out, and if you're using a calculator make sure you put in exactly the right number of noughts!

$$\text{Cheetah speed} = 100,000 \div 3,600$$
$$= 27.77777777777777777 \text{ m/s}$$

What a boring lot of 7s. As they come after the decimal point, we're allowed to knock most of them off and we find that cheetahs run at 27.78 m/s.

HANG ON! WHERE DID THAT '8' COME FROM?

The "8" comes from "rounding off" when you knocked off the 7s. Suppose we had let one more digit stay in place, we would have had 27.777. Instead we knocked the last "7" off, but the rule is, if the last digit you knock off is a five or bigger, it's a bit naughty just to ignore it completely, so you add one to the end digit of your new number. This gave us 27.78.

So much for cheetahs then. Next is the fast snail who can reach 50 metres per hour. Obviously a snail isn't as fast as a cheetah, but we'll do the conversion anyway. The distance is already in metres so we don't need to change that, but we *do* need to convert the hour to seconds. As we did before we divide by 3,600:

$$\text{Snail speed} = \frac{50 \text{ metres}}{3,600 \text{ seconds}} = 50 \div 3,600$$
$$= 0.0138888888888 \text{ m/s}$$

The eights look pretty dull too, so we'll lose most of them and round it off to find our turbo snail goes at a rather nifty 0.01389 m/s.

Finally, New York moves at 20 mm per year. Let's look at it:

$$\text{New York speed} = \frac{20\text{mm}}{1 \text{ year}}$$

First we have to change the 20 little millimetres to metres which comes out at 0.02 metres. Then we have to convert years to seconds. How many seconds are there in a year, eh?

There's 365 days in a year, times 24 hours in a day, times 60 minutes in an hour, times 60 seconds in a minute.

Multiply $365 \times 24 \times 60 \times 60$ to get 31,536,000 seconds in a year.

Of course, if you want to be a real pain, you now say this:

WHAT ABOUT A LEAP YEAR?
IT HAS 366 DAYS...

This is the sort of remark that makes maths teachers wish they'd gone to join a circus instead.

BETTER DO WHAT SHE SAYS, OR SHE'LL GIVE US EXTRA ALGEBRA HOMEWORK!

The fact is that unless you're the sort of saddo who really cares exactly how many cornflakes you ate for breakfast or how many bits of paper are on a toilet roll, then for sums like this, one extra day in a whole year doesn't matter.

Right then, back to New York. We divide the metres per year by the seconds to make a sum like this:

$$\text{New York speed in m/s} = \frac{0.02 \text{ metres}}{31536000 \text{ seconds}}$$

And when you divide that out you get: New York moves at 0.0000000006342 m/s.

At last! All five of our speeds are now in metres per second, so let's see how they compare.

70

Well surprise, surprise, light travels a lot faster than New York. Worth all the effort to find *that* out, wasn't it?

ONCE AGAIN WE INTERRUPT TO BRING YOU SOME IMPORTANT GOLLARK DATA: ONE GLOMP IS THE SAME AS 19 EARTH METRES. ONE MNULT IS THE SAME AS 3 EARTH DAYS

1 GLOMP = 19 METRES
1 MNULT = 3 DAYS

AS THE CRAFT CONTINUES TO ADVANCE WE CAN ONLY WAIT AND WONDER – WHAT ARE THE EARTH'S CHANCES OF SURVIVAL?..

RUMBBBBLE   RUMBBBLE

THE END IS NIGH

By now you'll be getting pretty scared about the Gollark invasion, so let's see how long we have to live. At least we've got enough information to work out the Gollark's speed in metres per second:

$$\text{Gollark speed} = \frac{180 \text{ glomps}}{1 \text{ mnult}}$$

Changing to m/s we get:

$$\text{Gollark speed} = \frac{180 \times 19 \text{ metres}}{3 \times 24 \times 60 \times 60 \text{ seconds}} = \frac{3,420 \text{ m/s}}{259,200}$$

If you work that out you find that the speed of the Gollark battle cruiser is 0.01319 m/s.

Hey! Just a minute, we've *already* found that snails move at 0.01389 m/s.

Good grief! Snails are slightly faster than the Gollark battle cruiser.

WE INTERRUPT YOU ONCE AGAIN TO BRING YOU INCREDIBLE DEVELOPMENTS IN THE GOLLARK SAGA...

IT SEEMS THAT NOT ONLY CAN SNAILS CATCH THE BATTLE-CRUISER...

EEEEk!

Earth is safe once again but it could have been a very different story – if only the Gollarks had known about murderous maths!

ONE-SIDED PAPER

Dear Sir,

I have just read the chapter heading in your book which says "One-sided paper". One-sided paper? Impossible! In all my years of teaching maths I've never heard of such rubbish. I have just two things to say to you:

1) You are a very silly man.

2) If I catch any of my pupils reading your ridiculous book, I'll make them darn my old brown hairy socks.

3) If you were in my class I would make you write out 10,000 times in very big letters "I must not waste paper".

Yours unimpressedly,

P. J. Blenkinsop

(A teacher with rotten handwriting)

Sorry Mr Blenkinsop, but you aren't going to like this much.

Let's think about a bit of normal plain paper. (Ooh yes please, that sounds *really* interesting.) It has two sides, hasn't it? And round the edge of the page is ... the *edge*! This is clever stuff, isn't it?

Just suppose a mad inventor had come up with "killer colour"...

HEH! HEH! ONE GLANCE AT THIS SEPTIC SHADE IS ENOUGH TO MAKE YOUR NOSE EXPLODE... AND I'VE DYED YOUR PIECE OF PAPER RIGHT THROUGH WITH IT!

You have to quickly paint the entire piece of paper black so that none of the killer colour shows at all. This is what you'd need to do:

1 Start on one side of the paper and work across to the edge.

2 When you get to the edge of the sheet, you'll have to go over the edge and then you will end up on the other side.

3 You can then black out the other side and eventually there won't be any killer colour left showing at all.

The important thing here is that to black out the entire sheet of paper, you have to go over the edge because the paper has two sides. However, if the piece of paper only had one side, you could black out the killer colour colour completely without going over an edge!

How to make a piece of one-sided paper

In the 1960s (i.e. when nobody had colour telly and hippy teachers had little flowers painted round their belly buttons) this sort of thing was called "modern maths". Now it's probably called ancient maths, but it's still a fun thing to do.

What you need are two long strips of paper. If you go shopping for *loads* of stuff at the supermarket, keep the till receipts because they are perfect for this. You also need some glue or tape.

1 Take one strip of paper and make it into a big circle by gluing the ends together. (As if you were making a big bracelet.)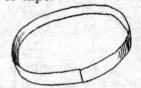

2 Do exactly the same with the other one, *but* before you stick the ends together, twist one end round so that it is upside down.

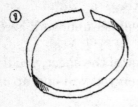 

This second circle is actually a one-sided piece of paper! If you want to be clever, it's called a *Möbius strip*, after the bloke who invented it.

76

1 Take your first circle, and draw a line along the middle of the strip until you get back to where you started. Because this strip has two sides, you'll find that one side has a line on, and the other hasn't.

2 Next, draw a line along your second circle and *keep going* until you get back where you started. Of course, what you'll find is that without going over the edge, you've drawn your line on what was both sides of the paper. The reason for this is that you've joined the two sides up, so the paper only has *one* side! If this second circle had been in "killer colour" you could have blacked it all out without going over the edge.

There's something else that's funny about this. One of your circles has two edges that go right round, but the other only has one! To prove this you need to find two trained ants who are madly in love.

Get your first paper circle and put one ant on each edge. Tell the ants that they can go and see each other, but have to walk along the edge to get there. What a mean trick – they'll never do it!

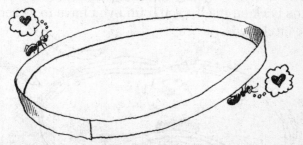

However, if you put your ants on each edge of the second circle, they can meet up by just walking along. This is because the two edges have joined up, and in fact the one-sided piece of paper only has one edge!

A magic trick

If you haven't got wobbly hands, go and get some scissors and try this. Take the first circle and cut along the line that you drew. (Be careful of the ants because they might have cheated and be snogging in the middle.)

When you've cut right round, not surprisingly you'll find that you've just divided your circle into two thinner circles. Of course if you chop anything down the middle, you divide it into two, don't you?

Now then, here's the weird bit – cut along the line you drew on your second circle. Even when you've divided the whole thing into two – what do you get?

If you're really interested in the strange things you can do with one-sided paper, here's another fun thing to do...

Make another circle with a twist in it (like your second circle from before). Instead of drawing a line along the middle, draw a line that's quite near the edge, and keep going until it goes right round and joins back on itself. (You'll find you have to go round the circle twice.)

Now then, can you guess what will happen when you cut along the line? Try it and see.

One final freaky illusion

Here's a Möbius strip trick to really amaze your friends – and even yourself!

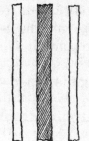

1 Get three long, thin strips of paper. They should all be the same length, but if one of them is slightly wider than the other two, so much the better. (If you're using three bits of supermarket till roll, you could trim two of them down very slightly.) Take the wider one and colour it in with a bright colour, like red.

2 Put them together with the wider one in the middle like a long sandwich. You'll find life is much easier later on if you use a few very small bits of Blu-tak to hold them together.

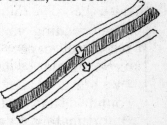

3 Put the ends of the sandwich together and add a twist, as if you were making a three-layered Möbius strip.

4 Stick the ends of the wider piece of paper together, and then stick the other loose ends together. You should have three separate joins when you are finished.

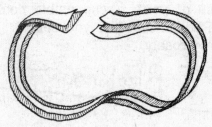

5 Show what you have made to a friend. Point out that there are two plain paper loops with a red loop in the middle separating them. As the red loop is slightly wider, you can see how it sticks out from between the two plain paper loops all the way round. Most importantly, there is no point at which the two plain loops touch!

6 Ask your friend – without tearing the paper – to pull the two plain loops away!

Dear Sir,

After reading your ridiculous chapter on one-sided paper I decided to try the experiments. I found two ants in love, and I've spent a year training them to walk round the edge of the paper. Unfortunately, I have discovered that ants only live for a few weeks and so it seems I have wasted many months talking to two dead ants, and trying to lead them round in circles with drops of honey on the end of a matchstick.

I am sure many more of your readers have done exactly the same as me because of your irresponsible book. You should be ashamed of yourself.

Yours crossly,

PJ Blenkinsop

STRANGE NUMBERS

"What can be strange about numbers?" you might say. Well, you wouldn't be the first.

The ancient Greek mathematician, Pythagoras, was very keen on trying to show that all sorts of things could be described by nice neat numbers. One particular example is the 3-4-5 triangle.

The 3-4-5 triangle

Ancient builders were always needing to measure "right angles", or in other words, square corners. One way of doing it is to have a set-square.

A set-square is fine for checking the angles on drawings, or little things like a cupboard or a box, but suppose you want to mark out the sides of a building? A set-square will be too small to be any use!

Right back in the days of ancient Egypt they found another way of doing it:

A ROPE WITH 12 EVENLY SPACED KNOTS

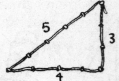

You get a rope and tie 12 knots in it at equal distances apart. You then arrange the rope in a triangle so that the sides are three spaces, four spaces and five spaces long. This will make a right-angled triangle! You can start with a rope as long as you like, providing your 12 knots are evenly spaced. By pulling your triangle tight it makes it easy to mark out a big right angle.

Pythagoras loved things that could be described by nice neat numbers such as three, four and five. It made life nice and simple and all his followers (called the Pythagorean Brotherhood) thought he was a really top bloke to hang out with. In fact they almost worshipped him when he came out with his biggest hit which was…

In case you don't know, a squared number is what you get if you multiply a number by itself, and you can write it down by putting a little "2" in the corner. For example: 6 squared is the same as 6^2 which means 6×6 and equals 36. Any number can be squared, such as $1,763^2$ which becomes 3,108,169. The easiest square is 1^2 because of course $1 \times 1 = 1$.

Right, now you know about squares, check out the triangle with sides measuring 3, 4 and 5 using Pythagoras's theorem. Pythagoras says that $3^2 + 4^2$ should equal 5^2. If you work the squares out you get $9 + 16 = 25$, so this one works!

Here are some more right-angled triangles to check...

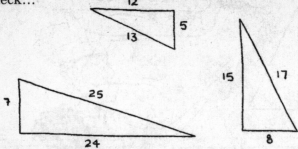

Anyway, back to Pythagoras and his Brotherhood who were all feeling rather pleased with life until one day...

This is where the trouble started. How long do you think the diagonal is?

- 2 m? (No … that's too long)
- 1 m? (No … that's too short)
- 1½ m? (Getting closer, but actually it's a bit too long)
- 1⅓ m? (Still close, but it's too short)
- 1⅖ m? (Getting very close, but actually too short)

Poor old Pythagoras tried for ages to find a way of describing how long the diagonal would be using fractions made up of his nice neat numbers, but it was never quite *exact*! This is because the answer is the first one of our strange numbers...

$$\sqrt{2}$$ The Square Root of **TWO!**

Do you like the fancy sign? It's just like the sort of thing you see when mad boffins write out monster equations ... but what does it mean?

It's actually easy to understand. Remember that a number squared means it is multiplied by itself. Suppose we had $2^2 = 4$, we can also say that 4 is the *square* of 2.

If you want to put it the other way round, you say the *square root* of 4 is 2 or you can put $\sqrt{4} = 2$.

Luckily, 4 is one of the numbers that has a nice neat square root, i.e. 2. Pythagoras would have liked that one! Unfortunately most numbers do not have a nice neat square root.

Can you see which of these numbers will have a neat square root?

$$1,2,3,4,5,6,7,8,9,10$$

The answer is, 1, 4 and 9 all have neat square roots. The others ... urgh!

Pythagoras's problem was that he wanted EVERY number to have a neat square root, even if it included a fraction. He wouldn't have even minded if the fraction was a really fancy one such as:

$$\frac{23}{36} \text{ or, } \frac{641}{1132} \text{ or even, } \frac{375837}{823391}$$

Just so long as he could put it in nice neat numbers.
The trouble is that he couldn't, and he got into
rather a murderous mood about it!

Pythagoras swore his brotherhood to secrecy, but of course even he couldn't pretend the square root of two didn't exist for ever. The trouble is that the square root of two (like most square roots) cannot be written out as a normal fraction. The only way to do it is as a long decimal fraction which starts:

1.41421356237 ... and the digits go on in a completely mixed-up order for ever!

The square root of three isn't any better. It starts 1.73205080756...

You might think a pleasant number like 10 has a nice square root, but no!

$$\sqrt{10} = 3.16227766017...$$

Strange numbers like this are called *irrational numbers*. It's a good name for them, because if you say someone is irrational it means they've gone a bit loopy, and that's why poor old Hippasus got shoved off the boat all those years ago.

Calculator tip!
On most calculators you can find the square of any number quickly by putting in the number then pushing "×" followed by "=", e.g. if you push 17× =you get 289, which is the same as 17×17.

If you want to find the square root of a number quickly, your calculator has to have a button marked with the square root sign $\sqrt{}$. Just put in the number then press the square root button, e.g. if you push 289 $\sqrt{}$ you will get 17.

You can have fun putting big numbers into your

calculator and guessing which ones will have nice neat square roots! Try these: 1,369, 3,141, 15,129, 36,333, 63,001.

There are many other irrational numbers which you can't write down exactly, and if you've read the chapter about measuring areas, you will have already have heard of the utterly fabulous pi.

Pi is a Greek letter written like this: π. Not much to look at, is it? Don't be fooled, π has become one of the most important numbers there is. In fact, it's *so* important that good calculators even have a special button for it.

Pi all started with the ancient mathematicians studying a simple circle.

And that is roughly how pi (or π) was born!

So, if you want to work out the circumference of a circle, all you need to do is measure the diameter then multiply by π, like this:

$$\text{Circumference} = \pi \times \text{Diameter}$$

Or, if you prefer a neat formula:

$$C = \pi D$$

Unfortunately for the ancients, they were stuck with just one *tiny* problem. They couldn't work out what π was!

To start with they used to say that the circumference was three times longer than the diameter, but they knew that was just a bit too short. The clever Greek, Archimedes, calculated it was about

$3^1/_7$, but he knew that wasn't *exactly* right.

In decimals $3^1/_7$ looks like: 3.142857142857142857 ... (Notice how the digits "142857" keep repeating even though they never come to an end.)

Although $3^1/_7$ is close enough for all but the most exact calculations, the actual value of π has been calculated by computers to be: 3.14159265358979323846... (Because π is an irrational number, here the digits never repeat in patterns, they just go on for ever.)

Eggheads and nuts
Here you can see π written out to 20 decimal places which is more than anybody would ever need. However, computer eggheads have calculated π to billions of decimal places – and if that wasn't pathetic enough, memory experts are always competing to see who can remember the most!

Pi recipes
Earlier on in this book you were promised some fancy formulas, well hold on to your pants because here they come!

These ones include π and also "r". The little "r" is the radius of a circle, which is how far it is from the middle of a circle to the edge. "r" is equal to half the diameter of the circle. In fact, if you want a *really* simple fomula just to start you off, you could have:

$$r = \frac{D}{2} \text{ or } r = D \times \frac{1}{2}$$

- You can also put this the other way round which is: $D = 2r$.
- We already know that the circumference of a circle $= \pi D$ or $2\pi r$.
- The area of a circle $= \pi \ (r \times r)$, or πr^2.
- The volume of a cylinder $= \pi r^2 \ h$.

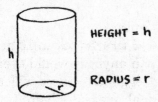

HEIGHT = h

RADIUS = r

- The volume of a sphere (or a round ball) $=$
$$\frac{4 \ \pi \ r^3}{3} \text{ or } \frac{4\pi \ (r \times r \times r)}{3}$$

- In fact anything that has a circle in it needs to use π in the formula!

Finally, here's a really hard formula that your maths teacher probably won't even know! If you chop the end off a ball, what is the volume of the end bit you chopped off?

CHOP THE END OFF...

h = HEIGHT
r = RADIUS

- The volume of the "cap" $= \dfrac{\pi h(3r^2 + h^2)}{6}$

Wahey! Now we're *really* talking murderous maths!

Be honest, have you understood all these formulas? If not, don't worry because that probably means you'll be better at something else in this book. However, if you *do* understand this complicated stuff then who knows? One day you and your super brain might dominate the universe.

MEANWHILE AT THE FREIGHT YARD...

Dolly was already waiting at the top of the stairs to the signal box as the six men arrived.

"Where's the big one?" she asked as they made their way up.

"He stayed back for lunch," replied Chainsaw. "And when Porky stays for lunch, there's no shifting him."

"I guess he's done his bit," admitted Dolly. "OK, inside you guys. There's someone you need to meet."

The signal box smelt of old oil and wood rot. A large display board covered one wall, while opposite was a massive window overlooking a maze of tracks and walkways.

"Gee, look at all the big levers," said Half-smile Gabrianni.

"They work the points and signals and stuff," grinned a small woman in a large boiler suit. "Pull one wrong and this whole place will pile up into a junk yard."

"Guys, meet Harri," said Dolly.

"Harry?" they all said.

"Harri as in Harriet," drawled the small woman. "Anyone want a chew of my spitting tobaccy?"

"No thank you kindly, ma'am," they muttered as they shuffled backwards into the far corner.

"So what's with the pretty lights?" asked One Finger Jimmy, pointing at the wall display with his one finger.

"This chart shows the rail track from here to Fort Knocks," said Dolly. "And the stops in between."

"And the lights show how the points are facing," said Harri. "As worked by me and my levers."

"OK, now listen up," said Dolly. "The Knocks Express leaves this yard tomorrow morning at 5.00 a.m. It travels at 30 miles per hour and reaches the Fort at 6.40 a.m. precisely. It'll be carrying 15 million bucks."

"Not to mention about 200 cops," said Blade.

"Not this one," said Dolly.

"No cops?" asked Chainsaw. "But what's to stop anybody just leaping aboard and grabbing a wad?"

"This 15 million is in coins," said Dolly.

"But that would take days to unload!" said Blade. "Supposing we stopped the train, how would we get it all away before the heat arrives?"

"Tell 'em, Harri," said Dolly.

"Five miles before Knocks, there's a set of points where an old mining track comes off the main line," said Harri, indicating the chart. "Those points are still good, and what's more I'm the only person who knows it."

"So all you have to do is take over the Express, run it down the mining track and hide it?" said Dolly.

"Yeah, and once the points are set back, I'll cut the cable," said Harri. "Nobody will ever find the train, so you can empty it in your own good time."

The men glanced at each other. It seemed too easy.

"OK, but how do we stop the train?" asked Jimmy. "I guess they don't pull up for hitchhikers."

"Yeah," agreed the Weasel. "And the old broken-down-car-stuck-across-the-line trick is so obvious they'll just plough right through it."

"Cattle," said Dolly.

"Cattle?" they asked.

"There's a cattle field right by the points," said Dolly. "Just before the train arrives you open the gate and herd them out across the line."

"But suppose the beefs get bored waiting and just wander off?" asked Blade. "Hell, none of us is cowboys, we can't keep them in place!"

"You'll just have to get your timing right, won't you?" said Dolly. "You'll have to work out exactly what time the train will be approaching."

"Oh no," said Blade. "Not *more* maths!"

THE STRANGE TALE OF MR FIELD & MR FENCE

Once upon a rustic time there were two odd gentlemen, Mr Field and Mr Fence. Sadly, though they were neighbours, they did not get on.

Mr Field owned a large patch of land, and Mr Fence owned a massive amount of railings. The problem was that Mr Field wanted some railings and Mr Fence wanted some land. They could not agree what was a fair exchange, and so they went to consult the magistrate.

"I suggest to you," said the magistrate, "that Mr Fence takes 100 metres of his railings, and puts them out on your land, Mr Field. All the land that his railings enclose will become his."

"And what do I get in return?" asked Mr Field.

"When you know how much land Mr Fence has acquired, you may mark out a piece of land of exactly the same area. Mr Fence will then be required to put railings around it, and those railings will be yours."

And so the deal was struck.

The following day Mr Fence arrived with exactly 100 metres of railings and set them out on Mr Field's land.

First he tried a rectangular shape.
"I've made a rectangle 40
metres long by 10 metres
wide," said Mr Fence.

"Therefore you have
enclosed an area of
40 × 10 metres," said the
magistrate. "Which is
400 square metres."

"Hmm," said Mr Fence. "Let me try again."

This time he made a shorter, fatter rectangle 30
metres long by 20 metres wide.

"Your area is now 30 × 20
square metres," said the
magistrate. "Which is 600
square metres!"

"Good grief!" muttered
Mr Field. "You mean with
the same railings, he can
enclose a different sized area?"

"It would seem so," agreed the magistrate.

"Let me try again," said Mr Fence.

This time he enclosed a perfectly square area
measuring 25 metres along
each side.

"Twenty-five by 25..."
muttered the magistrate
reaching for his calculator,
"gives 625 square metres!"

"Another 25!" moaned Mr
Field. "Surely the railings can't hold more?"

But Mr Fence had other ideas.

"I shall arrange my railings in a perfect circle,"

said Mr Fence.

The magistrate did the arithmetic.

"We know that the circumference of this circle is 100 metres," said the magistrate. He added solemnly, "And to work out the area, we need to use pi."

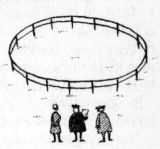

(Luckily the magistrate had read the last chapter of this book.)

How the magistrate worked out the area

1 First of all he worked out the radius of the circle using the formula:

$$\text{Circumference} = 2\pi r$$

2 Since he knew the circumference was 100 m, he wrote down: $100 = 2\pi r$.

3 Then he divided both sides of the equation by two to get: $50 = \pi r$.

4 Then he divided both sides of the equation by π to get: $\dfrac{50}{\pi} = r$

5 On his calculator he put in: $50 \div \pi$, and got the answer $r = 15.9$ metres.

6 The formula for the area of the circle is πr^2 so the magistrate entered $\pi \times 15.9 \times 15.9$ into his calculator and got the answer 795.

"Your area is now 795 square metres!" said the magistrate. "Let's call it 800 square metres and leave it there."

"That will be enough!" said Mr Fence. "I think that with this circular area I have reached my maximum."

"I should think so too!" exclaimed Mr Field. "This is monstrous!"

"Your turn, Mr Field," said the magistrate. "You may mark out an area of 800 square metres, and Mr Fence is obliged to fix railings all around it."

So Mr Fence marked out a plot of land measuring 20 metres along one side and 40 along the other.

"Twenty times 40 makes 800," said the magistrate.

"The area is correct."

"Two sides of 20 and two of 40 means I shall need 120 metres of railings," said Mr Fence.

"That sounds fair," said the magistrate.

"Just a minute!" said Mr Field as a cunning smile crossed his lips. "You did say the plot of land I marked out could be *any* shape?"

"Any shape," said the magistrate, "as long as the area is 800 metres."

Mr Field marked out a new plot.

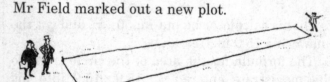

"There!" he said. "Ten metres by 80 metres, which is 800 metres."

"But that will need 180 metres of railing," said Mr Fence.

But Mr Field was not finished.

"Wait! I want to mark it again!"

Mr Field walked off into the far distance and marked out a very long thin area.

"One metre by 800 metres," said the magistrate. "Indeed, that does make for 800 square metres!"

"It makes for 1,602 metres of railings!" groaned Mr Fence.

"Still not enough!" said Mr Field leaping on his horse and riding off over the far horizon.

"Good grief!" said the magistrate, peering through some fabulously powerful binoculars. "The plot is now one millimetre wide by 800,000 metres long – but I am afraid the area is still only the 800 metres he is allowed!"

"I shall need 1,600,000 metres of railings!" wailed Mr Fence.

"And two millimetres for the ends," grinned Mr Field. "Now suppose I make it half a millimetre wide and twice as long again…"

This story is about areas and perimeters. (A perimeter is the line round the edge of an area. In the story the railings are acting like a perimeter round the field.)

You can have several things that have the same area, even though they are completely different shapes.

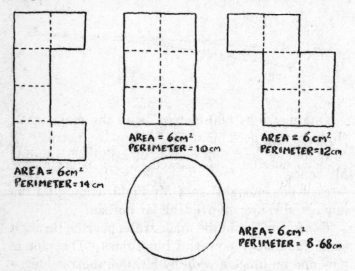

AREA = 6 cm²
PERIMETER = 14 cm

AREA = 6 cm²
PERIMETER = 10 cm

AREA = 6 cm²
PERIMETER = 12 cm

AREA = 6 cm²
PERIMETER = 8.68 cm

These three hexominoes are all the same area – you can see they each use up six squares measuring 1 cm × 1 cm on the page. The circle is also the same area.

However, as you can see, each of these shapes has a different length of perimeter.

SO WHAT ARE YOU GETTING AT?

All right, you asked for it.

If you have a fixed size of area, the smallest

perimeter you can give it is when your area is in a circle. If you want to be awkward like Mr Field in the story, a fixed area can have an unlimitedly big perimeter by making it very long and thin.

This area is also 6 cm² but the perimeter is really long. If the shape was even thinner, the perimeter could be even longer.

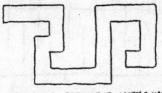

AREA = 6 cm² PERIMETER = VERY LONG

On the other hand, if you want to pack as much area as possible into a fixed length of perimeter, then make it a circle like Mr Fence did. Anything else gives you less area for your perimeter, it can even be so tiny as to be just about nothing.

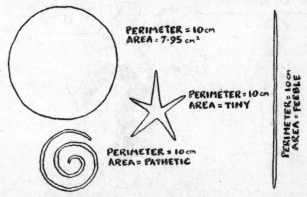

PERIMETER = 10 cm
AREA = 7·95 cm²

PERIMETER = 10 cm
AREA = TINY

PERIMETER = 10 cm
AREA = FEEBLE

PERIMETER = 10 cm
AREA = PATHETIC

How to climb through a postcard

Since we've sorted out areas and perimeters, it seems a good excuse to try this classic little stunt that looks impossible until you do it. Show a friend a postcard and say you can cut a hole in it big enough to climb through. Your friend is bound to think you're nuts, but here's how you cut the hole...

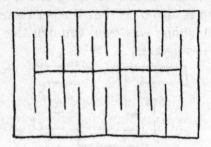

The card will open up into a long jagged circle which you should be able to step through!

THAT'S CLEVER... BUT WHAT'S IT GOT TO DO WITH MATHS?

WHO CARES? AT LEAST IT HASN'T GOT ANY SUMS IN IT!

MIRROR NUMBERS

A short chapter at the end of which we shall see a teacher's head short circuit

Mirror numbers (or "numerical palindromes" if you want to be posh) are numbers that are the same backwards as they are forwards such as 131 or 7227 or 2187812. What's strange about them is that there is a particular way of making them. Give this a try:

1 Pick a two digit number and write it down.
2 Underneath, write the same number back to front.
3 Add the two numbers together.
4 Underneath, write this answer back to front.
5 Add the two numbers together.
6 Keep doing this, and eventually you will make a mirror number!

Here's an example:

1 Start with 78.

2 Add,
$$\begin{array}{r} 78 \\ +87 \\ \hline = 165 \end{array}$$

3 Then,
$$\begin{array}{r} 165 \\ +561 \\ \hline = 726 \end{array}$$

4 Then,
$$\begin{array}{r} 726 \\ +627 \\ \hline = 1353 \end{array}$$

5 Then,
$$\begin{array}{r} 1353 \\ +3531 \\ \hline = 4884 \end{array}$$

6 There you are – 4884 is a mirror number!

OH NO! SEVEN YEARS' BAD LUCK!

- A lot of numbers come out much faster. Try 29:
$$29 + 92 = 121$$
- You can even start with a mirror number such as 55:
$$55 + 55 = 110 \text{ then } 110 + 011 = 121$$
- Warning! If you start with 89 or 98, the mirror number is 8813200023188.
- Just for fun you can challenge a friend. You each write down a two digit number, then give them to each other to work out. Whoever can get a mirror number from the starting number using the fewest sums, wins!
- If you're feeling *really* brave you can start off with numbers that have three or even more digits. Most come out quite easily, but no one has made a mirror number from 196 yet!

HOW TO BE FAMOUS FOR EVER!

FAMOUS FOR **EVER? REALLY?**

Oh yes.

Who do you think is famous now? Your favourite pop star? Somebody on the telly? Some sporty person? Big deal. In a few years' time most of them will be forgotten. Can you remember anyone who was famous last year? If you can, do you think they will still be famous in ten years? A hundred years? A thousand years?

Of course not, but maths can give *you* a chance to be famous for ever!

Back in ancient times mathematicians like Archimedes and Pythagoras solved some murderous problems and so they are still famous today. Luckily for us though, they left some problems still to do and if you could solve one of them, then you will still be famous in thousands of years' time!

KEVIN SMITH- MOST FAMOUS PERSON EVER!

Of course a lot of the unsolved problems are really tough, but there's one or two that look quite simple, including a couple in geometry which are just waiting to give you your big break.

SO WHAT'S GEOMETRY?

Good question, and by the most amazing chance you're about to find out.

SICK OF SUMS?
NAFFED OFF AT NUMBERS?
CRYING AT CALCULATORS?

THEN TRY

GEOMETRY!

IT'S FUN!   IT'S GROOVY!

JUST DRAW PATTERNS ALL DAY LONG!

"I NEVER KNEW MATHS COULD BE SO PRETTY"
MRS T. SQUARE   ESSEX

It's true. You get to do cute drawings and as an extra bonus, techno-nerds who rely on calculators will be completely stuck. It's even got a nickname – you can call it "geom" for short – which sounds like "jom".

Here's all you need for geom...

- a pencil
- a straight edge (such as a ruler)
- a pair of compasses for drawing curves and circles
- some paper.

So what's it all about?

Ancient mathematicians spent ages studying shapes such as circles and squares, and geom is the way of drawing these shapes and finding out how they all work together. The great thing is that the ancients never used numbers in pure geom, so you can ignore any markings on your ruler!

Here are a few geom tricks to get you started...

WARNING! You're going to be using a pair of compasses which have a sharp point. Make sure the paper you're drawing on is resting on something like an old phone book or a bit of thick cardboard. If the compass point goes through the paper and scratches up the dining-room table then you might be famous for another reason – having the angriest mum or dad in the world.

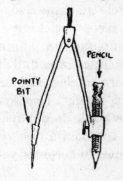

PENCIL

POINTY BIT

How to draw a circle

Utterly easy. Just stick the point of the compasses in the paper, open the pencil out a bit and then swizzle it round.

You have to draw a lot of circles and curves in geom which are exactly the same size, so once you've drawn a circle, don't open or close up your compasses until you've finished whatever else you're doing.

How to make flowery wallpaper

1 Draw a circle then keep the compasses open at exactly the same distance.

2 Stick the point of the compasses somewhere on the edge of the circle you just drew. Draw another circle the same size as the first.

3 Stick the point of the compasses in at a point where the two circles cross. Draw another circle the same size.

4 Keep sticking the compasses in wherever two lines cross and draw more circles. Colour in the "petals". Doodle in a 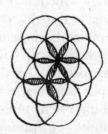 few stalks and maybe the odd leaf if you like.

5 In about a week you should have enough flowery paper to decorate your bathroom. Lovely.

How to chop a line exactly in half
This is called "bisecting" the line.

1 Draw a straight line (but don't get too fond of it because you're about to chop it in half).

2 Put the compass point in at one end of the line and open the compasses so that they reach just over half-way along the line.

3 Draw an arc (a bit of a circle) to cross the line.

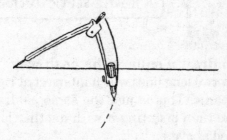

4 Keep your compasses set exactly the same distance apart, and stick the point in the other end of the line. Draw an arc which crosses the line and also crosses the first arc in two places.

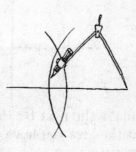

5 Use your straight edge and draw a line to join up the two places where your arcs cross.

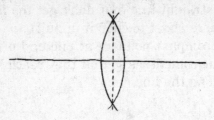

This new line not only divides the first line exactly in half, but the lines cross each other at an exact right angle. In other words they make a perfectly square corner, which is tremendously exciting. It means you can call your new line a perpendicular bisector.

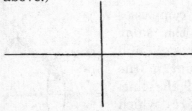

A PURPLE SEPTIC DOCTOR?

How to draw a square the posh way
1 Draw two long lines which intersect at right angles. (Don't panic. This is just the same as drawing one long line then bisecting it with another long line as described above.)

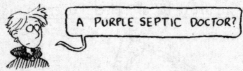

2 To make the next bit clearer, you might want to rub out the arcs you have drawn and just leave the lines.

3 Put the point of your compasses in where the lines cross and draw a circle.

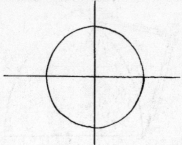

4 Join up the four places where the circle crosses the two lines.

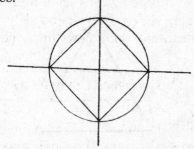

5 Hey presto – you just drew a perfect square!

How to draw an equilateral triangle

(A triangle with all three sides the same)

1 Draw a line, then stick the compass point in one end.

2 Open the compasses to the exact length of the line and draw a big arc upwards.

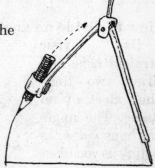

NOW THAT'S WHAT I CALL A BIG ARC!

3 Stick the compasses in the other end of the line and draw another arc crossing the first one.

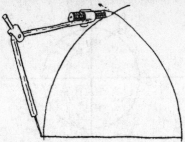

4 Draw two straight lines from where the arcs cross down to the two ends of the first line.

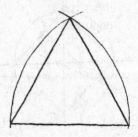

5 There you are – that's an equilateral triangle (which is probably easier to draw than to say).
By now you'll be itching to get famous, so there's just one more thing you might need to know.

How to divide an angle exactly into two

1 Use your straight edge and draw two lines that meet at an angle. The angle can be as wide or as pointy as you like.

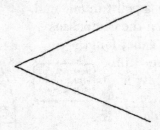

2 Stick the compass point in where the lines meet and draw an arc cutting the two lines.

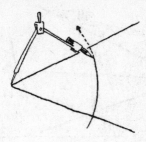

3 Stick the compass point in where the arc crosses one line and draw a second arc roughly in the middle of the angle. Keep the compasses open exactly the same distance!

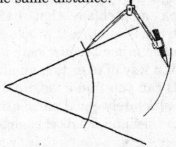

4 Stick the point in where the first arc crosses the other line and draw a third arc to cross through the second arc which you just drew in the middle of the angle.

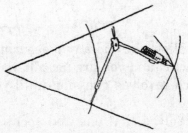

5 Draw a line from the point of the angle to where the second and third arcs meet.

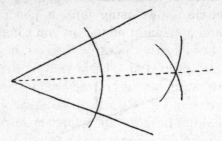

6 This new line *exactly* cuts the angle in half, regardless of how big the angle was to start with!

OK, that's enough playing about. By now you're ready to attack a problem that has baffled thousands of extremely intelligent people since time began! Brace yourself then because here it comes...

Can you invent a way of *tri*secting an angle?

In other words can you find a way to divide any angle into *three* absolutely equal parts using only a pencil, a straight edge and a pair of compasses?

IT SOUNDS EASY ENOUGH

SCRITCH SCRATCH

You are not allowed to do any measuring with a ruler or protractor, and you are not allowed to have a method which involves guessing until you get it right.

Once you've solved that one and spent the next

hundred years signing autographs and being on telly, here's another little teaser for you...

Draw a circle. Now, using only a pencil, your compasses and a straight edge, can you construct a square that has exactly the same area as the circle?

You might be interested to know that both of these problems are supposed to be impossible, but don't let that put you off. After all, ancient mathematicians couldn't programme a video or microwave chips, so maybe things have changed.

MEANWHILE IN A COW FIELD...

The herd stood silent in the pre-dawn gloom. In the distance two points of light made their way down the hillside towards it. Chainsaw peered through the windscreen of the Dodge sedan.

"This is as far as the track goes, Boss," he said. "I guess we're on foot from now."

"Kill the lights," snapped Blade. "Go on then, guys, you got beefs to shift."

The doors creaked open and a foot in a white leather shoe gingerly reached down to the ground.

"Feels kind of muddy," said Jimmy. "Where's the sidewalk?"

"There ain't no sidewalk, dummy," sneered Half-smile. "This is the country, see?"

"I don't know about see, but I sure can smell," said Jimmy. "And what I can smell is stuck to my shoes."

"Stop beefin'," said Blade. "Besides, we don't even know what time we're supposed to block the line."

"I was thinking about that," said the Weasel. "The train goes at 30 miles per hour, and we're five miles from the Fort, right?"

"That's what Doll said," said Blade.

"Well, if the train takes an hour to do 30 miles," said the Weasel, "then it don't take nearly so long to do five miles."

"Six fives are 30," said Numbers.

"Right!" said the Weasel. "So in one hour the train could do six lots of five miles."

"Why would it want to do that?" asked Blade.

"No, you don't get it," said Weasel. "I guess this train takes one sixth part of an hour to do the five miles."

"One sixth part of an hour – ten minutes!" said Numbers.

"There you are!" said Weasel. "The train will be passing here ten minutes before it's due to reach the Fort."

"Hey! It's due to reach the fort at 6:40," said Chainsaw.

"So ten minutes before that is 6:30," said Half-smile. "That's when the train's due past!"

"Guess you're all feeling pretty smart with your little bitty maths, huh?" said Blade.

In the darkness of the car, the others all grinned smugly.

"Well, I make the time 6:27," said Blade. "And my little bitty maths says you've got three minutes to wade through whatever these beefs have left on the ground and get them out on to that line, so *move it!*"

THE HUMAN PYRAMID

Wasn't it just the worst thing when you found your-self wandering alone across the arid wastes of the grand prairie? No wonder you were tempted to get a lift from the first people you saw, but no matter how desperate you were, you should have avoided getting into the lorry of Calamity Circus!

They haven't had a good season, and consequently every item of the circus is crammed into the back of one very miserable, overheated and unstable truck.

The engine whines and splutters as the truck makes its tedious way along a very bumpy path when *kar-rump!* the ground gives way and the whole lot falls down an abandoned mineshaft.

There you all are at the bottom of the shaft feeling grateful that you landed on the elephant and not the other way round. Far above you is a tiny patch of light showing the hole through which you fell. There are no ropes, ladders or indeed any other ways of climbing up. What do you do?

"Don't you worry!" says the ringmaster. "We can get somebody out, and they can bring help!"

"How can you get anyone out?" you ask.

"We can form a human pyramid!" he boasts. "Look!"

Immediately two acrobats stand together and a third leaps on to their shoulders.

"That's no good," you moan, "the hole is too far above us! We'll need a pyramid ten rows of people high."

"Ten rows of people, eh?" thinks the ringmaster. "The top row just needs one person, but the second row needs two and the third three and so on. The tenth row will need ten people. I don't know if we've got enough!"

How many people will the pyramid need?

The answer is $10+9+8+7+6+5+4+3+2+1$, which added up makes 55. However, rather than adding all the numbers up, there is a better way of working it out.

If you move the top of the pyramid over a bit, it makes a triangle like this:

0	0 0000000000
00	00 000000000
000	000 00000000
0000	0000 0000000
00000	00000 000000
000000	000000 00000
0000000	0000000 0000
00000000	00000000 000
000000000	000000000 00
0000000000	0000000000 0
Triangle	Two triangles

Look what happens if you put two identical triangles together! You get a rectangle. From this you can work out how many units are in your triangle!

1 First work out how many units are in the rectangle. Just count the units along the bottom (11) and multiply by the units up the side (10). This tells you that your rectangle has 11×10 which is 110 units in it.

2 Divide the total number of units by two to find out how many units are in each triangle:

$$110 \div 2 = 55!$$

(Because there are 10 rows in this triangle, the total "55" is called the 10th triangle number.)

You can find out the number of units in any triangle if you know how many rows there are. Just multiply the number of rows by the next number up, then divide by two!

The red balls on a snooker table always start in a triangle like this:

Can you see how many balls there should be? It's just: $5 \times 6 \div 2 = 15$.

Maths is full of nifty little short cuts and working out triangle (or pyramid) numbers is just one of them. One brilliant example occurred in a German classroom in 1786...

The teacher needed to nip out to get his wig powdered or something, so to keep the class quiet he said...

He was just putting his coat on and probably wondering if he had time to sneak in a quick sauerkraut butty in the local café while he was out, when a nine-year-old kid shouted out...

The teacher must have been utterly gobsmacked – but it was just his bad luck that the kid turned out to be Carl Friedrich Gauss, who went on to be a mental megastar. By the time he was 30 he had come up with tons of brainbusting stuff in maths and physics, so no wonder at the age of nine he could spot a short cut to triangle numbers. The answer was just: $1,000 \times 1,001 \div 2$, which works out pretty simply at 500,500. Anyway, there's no time to worry about Gauss right now because you're stuck underground with a travelling circus, remember?

"So we need 55 people," says the ringmaster, "we're in luck, we can do it!"

But just then the ground cracks open and everything falls down even further.

"We'll need 20 rows of people to make a pyramid high enough now!" you say. "The hole is twice as high as it was."

"So do we need twice as many people now?" asks the ringmaster.

"More than that!" you admit.

How many people does the pyramid now need?

Easy! $20 \times 21 \div 2 = 210$.

"Two hundred and ten people?" gasps the ring-master. "We can just do it if we use everybody, and because you worked it out, I'll give you a choice."

"What's that?" you say.

"In a pile of people 20 rows high, would you rather be on the top or the bottom?"

A curious (if useless) fact about triangle numbers

Look at the first ten triangle numbers:

- The first triangle number is 1.
- The second triangle number is 3.
- The third triangle number is 6.
- The fourth triangle number is 10.
- The fifth is 15, the sixth is 21, the seventh is 28, the eighth is 36, the ninth is 45, the tenth is 55 ... and so on.

(Triangle numbers can go on up as high as you like.)

Here comes that curious (if useless) fact...

You can make any number you like by adding together no more than three triangle numbers! (They don't have to be different, e.g. you can make 20 from $10 + 10$.)

- Suppose you want to make the number 64. Add $3 + 6 + 55 = 64$!
- How about making number 42? Add $36 + 6 = 42$
- Here are some to try yourself: 26, 38, 44, 49, 67.

You'll find some are trickier than others, but they can all be done!

The friendly way to work out triangle numbers

Suppose you wake up in the middle of the night panicking your pants off because you just have to know the seventh triangle number. You could multiply 7×8 and divide by 2 to get 28, but there is another way to do it.

You'll need:
- some bottles of lemonade and glasses
- some little sausages on sticks
- lots of crisps
- funny hats and crackers (optional).

What you must do is invite seven people round for an instant party. Now here's the important bit: when everybody has turned up, each person (including you) must shake hands once with every other person in the room. All you need to do is count the handshakes and that will give you the seventh triangle number.

This works for any number – so imagine you're in a train carriage with 13 other people and you suddenly desperately need to know the 13th triangle number. Get everybody to shake hands with you and each other and count up all the handshakes.

For fun you can try this the other way round. Suppose you are with a group of friends: count them all (but don't count yourself) and work out the triangle number. So if you're with four friends, the triangle number will be $4 \times 5 \div 2$ which is 10. Then tell them all how many handshakes it would be if you all shake – they'll be amazed that you could know before they've tried it!

THE PSYCHIC BLOBS

This is a great trick to play on a friend who thinks you're a bit sappy for reading a maths book. All you do is say that the book has been infested by the five psychic blobs of numerical ectoplasm which are on the next page. When your friend tells you that you are totally nuts, you can go ahead and prove it!

1 Ask your friend to pick a secret number between one and 30 without telling you what it is.

2 Your friend must now indicate which blobs have the secret number on.

3 Stare deeply at the psychic blobs, and explain that they are sending you a telepathic brain message.

4 You can now tell your friend the secret number!

5 Have a safe chair and a glass of water ready. Your friend will need them to recover from the shock.

So how does it work? Look at the numbers immediately above the eyes on each blob. Add together these numbers on the blobs your friend picks. (You'll see that some numbers such as "4" only appear on one blob, but others appear on more – i.e. "23" appears on four of them.)

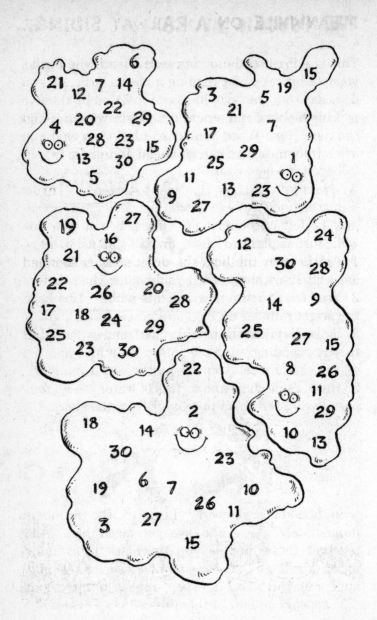

MEANWHILE ON A RAILWAY SIDING...

With a soft clang the points on the track slid back into place.

"I guess that's Harri pulling the lever in the signal box," said Half-smile. "So far so good, eh boss?"

"Come on," said Blade. "We got to get this train camouflaged before sun-up."

Blade watched as the men started to throw branches and leaves over the hijacked train. Somehow he felt uncomfortable – the job had gone too well. Just as planned, the train had stopped to allow the cattle over the line, the driver and stoker had even reversed it down the siding for them before leaping off and disappearing up the hill. The gang had practically been given 15 million dollars, albeit in coins. No, Blade didn't like it.

Chainsaw had found a small shutter in the side of one of the trucks.

"Boss," he called. "Look at this, it's come loose."

Blade joined the others who had gone to watch Chainsaw hit the metal panel with a stone. Suddenly it broke away and a stream of coins shot from the hole.

"Jackpot!" sniggered the Weasel.

"Quick, you dopes," hissed Blade. "We need something to catch it in!"

"Come here, Weasel," said Chainsaw. "We need your pants."

Weasel protested, but the others had already grabbed him and were holding him against the truck so that the coins flew down the back of his trousers.

"It's c-cold!" stammered Weasel.

"Get his necktie and tie it round his legs," said Blade. "We don't want the dough falling out at the bottom."

Gradually the flow of coins dwindled to a trickle then stopped.

"Hey, Weasel, you shrinking?" asked Jimmy.

"Not shrinking, he's sinking!" said Chainsaw.

134

Sure enough, Weasel, weighed down by his bloated trouser legs, was gradually slipping into the ground.

"Grab him!" ordered Blade. "There must be a fortune in his pants."

"Two thousand seven hundred and fourteen dollars," said Numbers. "I counted."

"We better make a start shifting this stuff," said Blade. "Carry him back to the car."

As they struggled past the roaming cows Weasel managed to gasp: "Hey Numbers, how many 2,714s are there in 15 million?"

"Five-five-two-six," said Numbers, "and a little bit."

"For the last time," snapped Blade, "will you guys quit with the maths?"

"But boss," moaned Weasel, "we got to think of a better system than this. Otherwise you guys will be lugging me across this cowfield five and a half thousand times."

"That's a lot of times," said Jimmy.

"I know how we could make it less times," said Chainsaw.

"How's that?" said Blade.

"We could buy Weasel some bigger pants."

THE TROLL'S CHALLENGE AND THE DEADLY ISLANDS OF DOOM

It's not your fault. It could have happened to anyone.

There you were, lightly skipping through Fairyglen Forest picking buttercups and daisies when you tripped on an old gnarled tree root and fell down a pit into the caverns of Neverworld.

You look around and see the walls are covered in strange mystic symbols. Just then you hear a muttered curse from a dank corner.

"No! It can't be done!" shrieks a voice.

"Then you must die!" cackles a mystic troll.

"Please … one more chance!" begs the voice.

It turns out that many years ago a peasant fell down the same pit and was caught by the troll. "Let me go," said the peasant, but the troll first set him a challenge.

"Choose one of the symbols on the wall," the troll had said. "Here is a long piece of string.

You must arrange the string in a pattern identical to the symbol, but you may not double the string back on itself at any point."

This is the symbol the peasant had chosen:

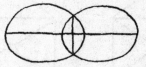

So, is the puzzle impossible, or is the peasant just a bit slow?

These puzzles are good fun (unless you're being threatened by a mystic troll).

Rather than use a piece of string, usually you're asked to draw a diagram but:

● you must not take your pen off the paper.
● you must not go over any line twice.

The classic example is called the envelope puzzle because it looks like the back of a closed envelope:

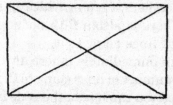

Can you draw this diagram without taking your pen off the paper, and without going over any line twice?

The answer is NO.

Note: If some big-head tells you he can do it, then he's cheating. The only way he can do it is either by folding the paper over, or by rubbing a line out afterwards or by having a wonky pen that doesn't write sometimes. Remember that people like that usually don't have any friends and tend to get their hands stuck in vending machines.

Now then, look at this open envelope...

 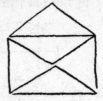

By starting at one of the bottom corners and finishing at the other, you can draw it!

How can you tell if you're going to be able to draw a pattern without taking your pen off the paper?

The secret is to look at all the places where lines join up. (These are called *nodes*.)

The closed envelope has five nodes. Four of them are the four corners, each of which has three lines going to it. There is also a fifth node in the middle which has four lines going to it.

Now you can immediately ignore any nodes which have an even number of lines going to them, so for the closed envelope you can ignore the node in the middle. What you need to know is how many nodes have an *odd* number of lines going to them, i.e. 1,3,5, etc.

● The closed envelope has *four* odd nodes (each with three lines).

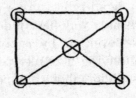

Now, if you look at the open envelope, remember you can ignore any nodes with an even number of lines, so:

- The open envelope has *two* odd nodes.

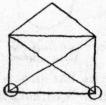

Now get this: You can draw any picture without taking your pen off the paper if there are two odd nodes or less.

Special node notes
- If a picture has no odd nodes, you can start and finish where you like.
- If there are two odd nodes, you have to start at one and finish at the other.

In other words, you could draw this picture if you wanted:

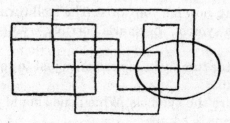

It has only two odd nodes. (Can you find them?)

Before we go back to Neverworld, there are two more things to know.

1 If you have a line sticking out, then the end of the line is counted as an odd node.

Look at these:

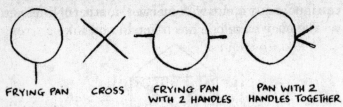

The first frying-pan has *two* odd nodes, so you should be able to draw it without taking your pen off the paper.

The cross has *four* odd nodes so you will have to take your pen off the paper. As for the pans with two handles ... work it out yourself, it's dead easy.

2 You can only have an even number of odd nodes! That's because a line always has to have two ends. Try it ... scribble a few lines together then count up the odd nodes. There *has* to be an even number.

So back to Neverworld ... look at the symbol the peasant chose. How many odd nodes are there?

Anyway, now it's your turn. The troll turns to you.

"Pick a symbol," he snarls horribly, trying to scare you.

"Tum tee tum," you say casually, just to get him all wound up.

Here are the symbols. Which one should you pick if you want to escape?

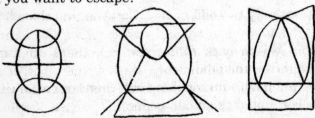

Of course being dead clever you pick the right symbol and get out of Neverworld, but then as you speed away from Fairyglen Forest you take a wrong turn and find yourself in...

The foul city of Fastbuck

In the middle of the city (near Putrid Park) is the disgusting Lake Nasty. Over the years all the filth from the city has been poured into the lake, and all the radioactive and biological waste has been piled up on three islands called Yuk, Ug and Poo.

The islands are linked to the mainland and each other by eight bridges as you can see on this map:

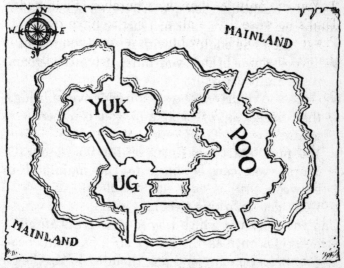

Suddenly one dark and smelly night the entire city is awoken by an awful groan. It seems the mixture of waste on the islands has started to mutate! It is forming itself into hideous Crud creatures who will forever roam the land bringing disease, famine, plague and extra French homework to everyone.

The only way to avert this disaster is to destroy the bridges. Naturally, being a hero, you immediately volunteer. These are your instructions:

- You are to be equipped with a giant steamroller.
- To destroy a bridge you must drive the steamroller right across it.
- Once you've driven the steamroller over a bridge, that bridge is wrecked and you can't cross it again.
- You must start and finish on the mainland. (Of course you can go back to the mainland in between, too.)
- Don't get a parking ticket.

Can you work out which way to go to cross *all* eight bridges just once each? (Better still, pass this book to your worst enemy and ask them to do it. They'll be there *for ever*!)

After some hours of driving around and squashing everything in sight with your giant steamroller, you will start to realize that this task is impossible. There

142

will always be at least one bridge left standing, and you might end up stuck on one of the islands as well.

Just as you are about to give up, a batty billionaire suddenly says, "Would it help if I quickly built an extra bridge?"

The citizens of Fastbuck all *groan*.

"We want the bridges knocked down," says the mayor, "we don't want any more!"

"Well, if the steamroller went over my new bridge, it would get knocked down just like the others..." explains the billionaire.

The crowd all start to mutter words like "thickie" at the billionaire, but then...

Flash! A giant light bulb suddenly comes on in your brain as you realize this is the same sort of challenge as the one you faced in Neverworld.

If you are brainy then stop reading! Can you work out how an extra bridge could help you?

Look at the map of the bridges. You have to go over each one once with no doubling back, just like when you were drawing the troll's mystic symbols.

To make it clearer, the first thing to do is to draw a diagram of all the bridges like this:

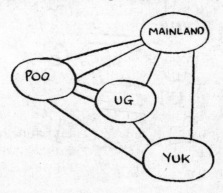

The lines represent the bridges. For example, there are two bridges going from the mainland to Poo, so there are two lines on the diagram. There is only one bridge going from Ug to Yuk, so the diagram only has one line, and so on.

You can treat the diagram like one of the Troll's mystic symbols because the islands (and the mainland) are nodes! Immediately you can see that there is an even number of lines going to Ug and the mainland and an odd number of lines going to Yuk and Poo. This means that you have two *odd* nodes! If you look back a few pages and check the "Special node notes" you'll see that it *is* possible to drive over all the bridges once *but* you have to start on Yuk and finish on Poo. (Try it!)

The trouble is that you have to start and finish on the mainland or the putrid Crud creatures will get you. Check the "Special node notes" again. They say you can start and finish where you like if there are no odd nodes. This is where the batty billionaire comes in.

Suppose you put an extra bridge between Yuk and Poo...

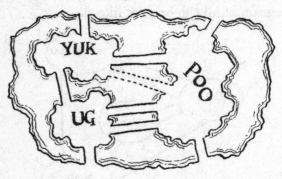

This means Yuk and Poo now both have an *even* number of bridges going to them, so they are not odd nodes any longer. In fact you haven't got any odd nodes now, so you can start and finish wherever you like. That means you can start and finish on the mainland, which is what you want.

Try it out! You should now be able to destroy *all* the bridges (including the new one) and get back to the mainland in time to save the city from the creatures of Crud.

THE GREAT RHUN OF JEPATTI AND THE SQUARES OF MYSTERY

MANY THOUSANDS OF YEARS AGO IN A MOST DISTANT LAND THERE DID ONCE LIVE THE GREAT RHUN OF JEPATTI. THE RHUN WAS THE RICHEST RULER THAT EVER GOVERNED THE GOLDEN JEPATTI PROVINCES, AND THE TALE OF HIS FABULOUS WEALTH IS TOLD AS FOLLOWS...

The palace of the Rhun had 60 great chambers, and in each lived one of the Rhun's illustrious sons – each chamber, that is, except one. The Rhun had only been blessed with 59 heirs before his wife decided the ancient washing machine couldn't cope and announced, "No more!"

And so it came to be that in one chamber dwelt not a son but the Ghinji, a loathsome three-tongued serpent and devourer of human flesh.

Over the years many families visited the Rhun and presented their finest daughters for marriage. On payment of a rich dowry, the prospective bride would be allowed to choose a chamber, and enter therein. The Rhun promised that on finding a son, he would hold the wedding the very next day.

Yet on finding the Ghinji, the door would be closed and the dowry forfeit to the Rhun.

And, dear reader, here lies the mystery: in all the time that passed, not one bride did end in marriage, but rather all came to rest in the belly of the Ghinji.

BURP!

BOTHER!

Wow! Gruesome story, eh? But how did the Rhun swing it? How come every bride met up with the Ghinji? The secret is down to how they had to choose a room.

The doors to the 60 rooms were numbered from 1 to 60, and the prospective bride was shown a great tablet of stone on which was inscribed the ancient "square of mystery".

COOL!

11	12	8	9	10
8	9	5	6	7
12	13	9	10	11
3	4	0	1	2
10	11	7	8	9

The bride was invited to choose one number from the square and this number was marked with a circle round it. Next, all the numbers in the column above and below were crossed out, and all the numbers in the same line going across were crossed out too. Suppose she picked the 13 on the third row, this is what it would look like:

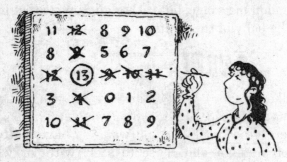

She then had to choose any other number that was not crossed out – e.g. the "1". Again a circle went round it and the numbers in the same row and column were crossed off.

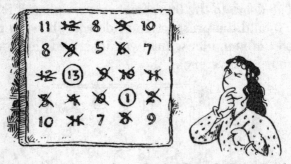

Following the same rules, she had to choose another number (e.g. the "10" on the bottom line). She would then be left with four numbers to choose from (let's say she picked the "8"), and finally there would be one uncrossed number left which was circled also. In this example it would be the "7".

148

The circled numbers were added up to give the number of the room she had to go into. In this case, if you add up $13 + 1 + 10 + 8 + 7$ you get 39.

Here's the spooky bit – it wouldn't have mattered which number she chose to start with, or which numbers she chose as she went along – the answer was always 39!

Suppose she picked the "6" to start with, and after that the "7" on the bottom line, then the "4", then the "12" on the left-hand side...

YUMMY!

You'll see that the only number left is the "10" at the top. Add them up: $6 + 7 + 4 + 12 + 10 = 39$!

No wonder the Rhun was so rich. All he had to do was make sure his Ghinji was behind door 39 and ready for lunch.

How to make your own mystery squares

You can make mystery squares produce any number you like, and so they are a great trick to play on your friends – and if you have 59 illustrious sons and a Ghinji, then you could make a walloping stack of money too. It takes a little bit of practice, but it's well worth it because when you get it right you'll find you can do it quickly and really amaze people.

All you need to start with is an empty grid with 25 squares in it, a pen and a friend called Patsy.

GRID   PEN   PATSY

Ask Patsy what mystery number she would like, and write it down. She can choose *any* number over 20 (but don't let her go too high or it gets trickier). Let's say Patsy chooses 27.

First of all let's make *the simple version* of the mystery square:

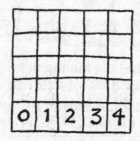

150

1 Start by putting 0, 1, 2, 3, 4 along the bottom line. OK, now here comes the bit which needs practice...

2 Subtract ten from Patsy's number – so if she gave you the number 27, you would get the answer 17.

3 You have to split this number into four smaller numbers – so for 17 you could have 2,3,5,7 because $2+3+5+7=17$. (It doesn't matter what the four numbers are so long as they are different and they add together to make 17.) Try to do this in your head.

4 Put these four numbers in the column above where the zero is. They can be in any order.

7				
2				
5				
3				
0	1	2	3	4

5 Fill in the rest of the grid by "counting along". For example, starting with the 7, just put in 8, 9, 10, and 11.

7	8	9	10	11
2	3	4	5	6
5	6	7	8	9
3	4	5	6	7
0	1	2	3	4

151

There – you've done it! You can now ask Patsy to choose whichever numbers she likes and as she does so, you circle them and cross out the other numbers in the lines and columns they are in. The five circled numbers at the end will always add up to 27!

If you make your mystery square big enough, instead of crossing the numbers out with a pencil, you can cover them over with counters (or coins if you're rich). This means that once you have made and tried out your mystery square, you can tip the counters off and ask Patsy to pick some different numbers – and again the total will be 27! This will *really* fool her.

Right, now that you can make the simple version of the mystery square, it's time for the even more baffling *complicated version*.

All we're doing here is mixing it up so that we get rid of the row along the bottom going 0,1,2,3,4. If Patsy sees that she might start to suspect how you did it, so here's a way to really fool her.

1 Before you start you can ask Patsy to choose *any* square she likes and you will put a zero in it.

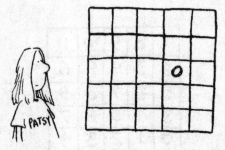

2 As soon as you've put in the zero, you fill in the

numbers 1,2,3,4 on the same line in any order.

3 Next you work out the other four numbers you need as before. Let's say this time Patsy picked 41 as her number. As before the first job is to subtract 10, which leaves 31.

4 Now we break the 31 up into four different numbers. How about this: $11+5+7+8=31$. This means the four numbers we'll use are 11, 5, 7 and 8.

5 Fill these numbers in any order above and below the 0.

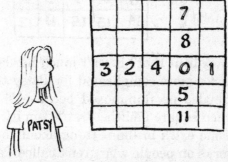

6 Fill in the other numbers counting as before, but put them in above (or below) the 1, 2, 3 and 4 in order. For example, look at the top line of the grid below. You'll see the number above the 0 is a 7 and so all the other numbers on the line count up from 7. This means the number above the 1 is 8, the number above the 2 is 9, the number above the 3 is 10 and the number above the 4 is 11.

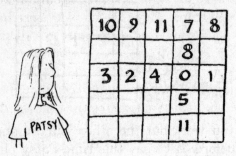

10	9	11	7	8
			8	
3	2	4	0	1
			5	
			11	

Here's the completed mystery square for number 41:

10	9	11	7	8
11	10	12	8	9
3	2	4	0	1
8	7	9	5	6
14	13	15	11	12

There! How about that? It isn't much harder to do, but it is a *lot* more complicated for Patsy to figure out. She'll also be flummoxed because she could choose which square had the first "0" on it!

There's one extra brilliant thing about this trick. It even works on people who aren't called Patsy!

MEANWHILE IN LUIGI'S DINER...

Benni hovered nervously behind the counter. He recalled the shady figures seated around table 12 all too well. Last time they had visited, there had been a serious lead shower and there were still stains on the floor that he had to explain away as spilt tomato sauce. People had got to thinking he was the clumsiest waiter in town. Mind you, thought Benni, this time they were sitting with a classy dame so maybe they were on their best behaviour.

"There it is, Doll," said Blade. "One banker's cheque for all the bail money, plus interest."

"You did well, guys," said Dolly folding the cheque and slipping it into a secret trapdoor in one of her high heels.

"It was tough work getting all that dough to the bank," said Half-smile.

"You don't say," sniggered Doll. "By the way, Weasel, what's the matter with your pants? I seen smaller circus tents."

"Don't ask," replied the Weasel, who could just about see over the belt buckle of his gargantuan trousers.

"So now we've paid our dues," said Blade, "we'll be on our way."

"What's the hurry, boys?" asked Dolly. "Don't you want to know who this cheque is going to?"

The gang looked at each other uneasily, but then the door opened.

"Evening, boys," said the prison governor. "Long time no see!"

"It's the Beak!" gasped Chainsaw.

"Relax," said Blade. "We're all paid up. He can't touch us."

"You paid, huh?" sneered the governor. "Is that right, Doll?"

"Not a cent, honey," said Dolly who had gone over to close the door behind him.

"Is that a fact?" said the governor. From inside his coat he pulled a nine-barrelled Dawson-Roach 25-bore multi-target self-loading hydraulic action scatter cannon. "Oh mother of mercy!" whimpered Half-smile.

"Eight-fifty slugs a second," muttered Numbers. "Nice piece."

"The way me and Doll see it," drawled the governor, "you seven saps skipped bail and word has it you turned over the Knocks Express. Boy, are they going to give you a welcome at Grimstate."

"I knew it was a double-cross," said Blade. "I knew we'd never get bail even at ten million. And the engine crew parking the train, then running away just like that..."

"Harri's brothers," said Doll. "We didn't leave nothing to chance."

"Face it, guys," sighed Blade. "Doll and the Beak have fixed us real good."

"You always were a loser, Blade," said Dolly. "When you're back inside taking the rap, me and the Beak will be taking a long flight."

"Just tell me one thing," said Blade. "Who chucked the dynamite into the cell?"

The governor smiled.

"I got to take credit for that. You guys were getting it too easy in there, I figured you needed encouraging to get out more."

Dolly called over to Benni.

"Hey, you behind the counter. Pull down the shutters. This place closes early tonight."

Benni hurriedly obliged.

"And when you've done that, go call the Feds," said the governor. "In the meantime, just one of you has to twitch and *kapow*, you're all bolognese sauce."

Whump! The door suddenly burst off its hinges and landed on the floor, completely sandwiching Dolly and the governor underneath. A massive figure staggered inside.

"It's Porky!" gasped the gang.

"Am I too late?" puffed the figure who had come to a halt standing on the door. "I was just coming for dinner and I saw the place closing up early. I figured if I was quick I might just make a late order, and so I was running but the door was shut and when I'm moving fast I don't stop so good and gee, I'm sure sorry about the damage, Benni."

From under the door came some muffled groans.

"Porky," ordered Blade. "Don't move your feet from

that spot. Jimmy, shove him a chair. The rest of you guys, move the table right up to him. Benni, you go and get three of everything on that menu and put it out in front of my biggest and bestest buddy here."

"But boss," said Porky, "I can't afford three of everything."

"That's OK, big man," grinned Blade. "Tonight you're having dinner on the Beak."

Three hours later the party was still going on.

"...and you know what the best part is," said Blade. "The Beak came in here to arrest a gang of seven men – but he didn't realize there was only six of us here!"

Indeed, if only the governor had stopped to count them up the story would have ended very differently. It just goes to show, even the simplest maths can be murderous.